New Directions for Community Colleges

Arthur M. Cohen
EDITOR-IN-CHIEF

Florence B. Brawer
ASSOCIATE EDITOR

Carrie B. Kisker
MANAGING EDITOR

Benchmarking: An Essential Tool for Assessment, Improvement, and Accountability

Jeffrey A. Seybert
EDITOR

Number 134 • Summer 2006
Jossey-Bass
San Francisco

BENCHMARKING: AN ESSENTIAL TOOL FOR ASSESSMENT, IMPROVEMENT, AND ACCOUNTABILITY
Jeffrey A. Seybert (ed.)
New Directions for Community Colleges, no. 134

Arthur M. Cohen, Editor-in-Chief
Florence B. Brawer, Associate Editor

NEW DIRECTIONS FOR COMMUNITY COLLEGES (ISSN 0194-3081, electronic ISSN 1536-0733) is part of The Jossey-Bass Higher and Adult Education Series and is published quarterly by Wiley Subscription Services, Inc., A Wiley Company, at Jossey-Bass, 989 Market Street, San Francisco, California 94103-1741. Periodicals Postage Paid at San Francisco, California, and at additional mailing offices. POSTMASTER: Send address changes to New Directions for Community Colleges, Jossey-Bass, 989 Market Street, San Francisco, California 94103-1741.

SUBSCRIPTIONS cost $80.00 for individuals and $180.00 for institutions, agencies, and libraries. Prices subject to change. See order form at the back of book.

EDITORIAL CORRESPONDENCE should be sent to the Editor-in-Chief, Arthur M. Cohen, at the Graduate School of Education and Information Studies, University of California, Box 951521, Los Angeles, California 90095-1521. All manuscripts receive anonymous reviews by external referees.

New Directions for Community Colleges is indexed in Current Index to Journals in Education (ERIC).

Microfilm copies of issues and articles are available in 16mm and 35mm, as well as microfiche in 105mm, through University Microfilms Inc., 300 North Zeeb Road, Ann Arbor, Michigan 48106-1346.

CONTENTS

EDITOR'S NOTES

Within the last two decades, institutions of higher education have come under increased pressure to become more accountable to their various constituencies, including regional accrediting agencies, state governing boards and legislatures, business and industry, and the general public. Indeed, as Banta (1999) notes, "Never before has higher education been subjected to such close scrutiny by public stakeholders" (p. 1). In response to this scrutiny, community colleges and other institutions have created initiatives to assess institutional effectiveness and student learning outcomes. Such quality assessment efforts in the community college sector include the League for Innovation in the Community College's Institutional Effectiveness Task Force and accompanying monograph (Doucette and Hughes, 1990) as well as their Learning Outcomes for the 21st Century project (Wilson, Miles, Baker, and Schoenberger, 2000); the American Association of Community College's *Core Indicators of Effectiveness for Community Colleges* (Alfred, Ewell, Hudgins, and McClenney, 1999); and the National Center for Higher Education Management System's monograph, *Assessment in Community Colleges: Setting the Standard for Higher Education* (Banta, 1999).

Implied in these initiatives is the expectation that, at some point, colleges will be able to focus externally and gauge themselves against similar data from comparable peer institutions. Until recently, however, few data collection and reporting processes were available to help community colleges gather information on comparable peer institutions on a national basis. In the last few years several new initiatives to collect and share data across the two-year college sector have been designed and implemented. This volume of *New Directions for Community Colleges* highlights four of these initiatives. These four were selected because they represent relatively new efforts designed specifically for community colleges and because they focus on areas of particular interest to two-year institutions. All four initiatives are in different stages of development and have been designed in very different ways. For example, one of the initiatives highlighted in the volume—the Kansas Study of Community College Costs and Instructional Productivity—involves data that primarily address institutional efficiency, while the other three address institutional effectiveness. As well, the Noel-Levitz Student Satisfaction Inventory and the Community College Survey of Student Engagement were designed to produce data that are statistically representative of community colleges nationwide and can therefore be generalized to that population. They can thus be characterized as having

NEW DIRECTIONS FOR COMMUNITY COLLEGES, no. 134, Summer 2006   © Wiley Periodicals, Inc.
Published online in Wiley InterScience (www.interscience.wiley.com) • DOI: 10.1002/cc.231

relevant statistical properties such as reliability and validity, and their data are appropriate to analyze for determination of such things as significant difference and effect size. The other two projects—the Kansas Study of Community College Instructional Costs and Productivity and the National Community College Benchmark Project—are in much earlier stages of development and are currently working to increase the size of their institutional participant dataset. In fact, since the underlying purpose of the two latter projects is to enable participating colleges to select groups of comparable peer institutions and benchmark against them, issues of representativeness and specific statistical properties of the data collected and reported may not even be relevant. Additional information regarding these issues may be found on individual project Web sites.

This volume is comprised of four major sections, each with two chapters. The first chapter in each section introduces and describes one of the four initiatives and is authored by individuals directly involved with the design or implementation of that project. The second chapter in each section describes how a participating institution or state system used data from that initiative, paying particular attention to ways in which the data and information were used for assessment, benchmarking, institutional improvement, planning, management, and decision making. This volume exposes readers not only to these relatively new, innovative national data collection and benchmarking consortia, but also to best practice examples of how data and information from these four initiatives have been used.

The volume begins with the initiative addressing institutional efficiency, the Kansas Study, then presents the three initiatives that primarily address institutional effectiveness. In Chapter One, Patricia Sumner and Regina Brewer describe the design, development, and implementation of the Kansas Study of Community College Instructional Costs and Productivity, an annual nationwide examination of how much full- and part-time community college faculty teach and at what cost. In Chapter Two, George Malo and Ellen Weed report ways in which Kansas Study data are used for program improvement and regional accreditation requirements in individual institutions and state systems.

In Chapter Three, Julie Bryant describes the content, development, and implementation of the Noel-Levitz Student Satisfaction Inventory (SSI) and explains its importance and utility for community colleges. She discusses ways in which the SSI can assess student experiences both inside and outside the classroom and how it can provide a campuswide assessment of institutional strengths and challenges. In the following chapter, Anne Kress recounts how Santa Fe Community College, using information provided by the SSI, has been able to identify student priorities and target initiatives in areas of importance to students. She describes how, through regular assessment, repeated review and dissemination of results, and an active commitment to institutional improvement, the college has implemented programs leading to marked increases in student satisfaction.

Chapter Five, by Kay McClenney, offers an overview of the Community College Survey of Student Engagement (CCSSE), and describes its five benchmarks of effective educational practice. Using CCSSE reports and data search tools, community colleges can benchmark their performance on key indicators related to teaching, learning, and retention. In Chapter Six, Scott Balog and Sally Search describe how Tallahassee Community College, through faculty workshops to discuss the results of CCSSE and state accountability data, implemented a quality enhancement plan involving careful assessment of data, research into best practices, and extensive faculty involvement.

Chapter Seven, written by Ralph Juhnke, describes the design and development of the National Community College Benchmark Project (NCCBP), which collects and reports a wide array of data on community college instruction, student outcomes, workforce development, minority participation, distance learning, faculty workloads, cost, and human resources, and which allows live, real-time peer selection and benchmarking. In Chapter Eight, Terri Manning and Brad Bostian discuss how Central Piedmont Community College has used NCCBP data to learn about and work to improve its retention and course withdrawal rates.

Benchmarking can be an essential tool for community college assessment and improvement. However, benchmarking is not without its share of challenges. Chapter Nine, written by Trudy Bers, outlines the limitations of both the process of benchmarking and the resulting benchmarks themselves. The volume concludes with a chapter by Caroline Sheldon and Nathan Durdella, who provide a list of resources and information on community college benchmarking that will be useful to practitioners eager to implement the practice at their own institution.

Institutions considering the use of benchmarking and benchmarks should understand the ways in which they are different from locally developed assessments of efficiency and effectiveness. For example, locally developed assessments can reveal much about the strengths and weaknesses of an institution and provide a rich source of data and information on which to base continuous improvement efforts. Those assessments cannot, however, provide any information about institutional quality in the larger context; that is, how successful the college has been in relation to its major goals and activities. That type of information can only come from an external examination of the college through comparisons with peer institutions and benchmarking.

Finally, it is important that colleges understand the costs involved in participating in peer comparison and benchmarking initiatives. In some cases there are real monetary costs—for example, enrollment or participation fees may amount to several thousand dollars per year. In all cases there are human resource and workload costs. All benchmarking initiatives require careful collection and reporting of data by participating institutions. The degree of the data collection and reporting burden will depend on the sophistication of the institution's management information system and the ability of institutional research (or other) staff to extract data from that system. In any case, colleges need to be aware of these costs and take them into consideration before embarking on a benchmarking project. That said, participation in peer comparison and benchmarking initiatives such as those described in this volume can greatly enhance a community college's efforts to improve teaching and learning, policy development, and planning and management. The institutional benefits resulting from participation in projects such as these far outweigh their inherent costs.

Jeffrey A. Seybert
Editor

References

Alfred, R., Ewell, P., Hudgins, J., and McClenney, K. *Core Indicators of Effectiveness for Community Colleges* (2nd ed.). Washington, D.C.: Community College Press, 1999.

"America's Best Colleges, 1996." *U.S. News and World Report,* Sept. 19, 1996, pp. 91–105.

Banta, T. W. *Assessment in Community Colleges: Setting the Standard for Higher Education.* Boulder, Colo.: National Center for Higher Education Management Systems, 1999.

Doucette, D., and Hughes, B. *Assessing Institutional Effectiveness in Community Colleges.* Laguna Hills, Calif.: League for Innovation in the Community College, 1990.

Wilson, C. D., Miles, C. L., Baker, R. L., and Shoenberger, R. L. *Learning Outcomes for the 21st Century: Report of a Community College Study.* Mission Viejo, Calif.: League for Innovation in the Community College, 2000.

JEFFREY A. SEYBERT is director of research, evaluation, and instructional development at Johnson County Community College in Overland Park, Kansas, and project director for both the Kansas Study of Community College Instructional Costs and Productivity and the National Community College Benchmark Project.

1

This chapter discusses the development and implementation of the Kansas Study of Instructional Costs and Productivity, which collects and reports data on community college instructional costs and faculty workloads. The project provides data for both intra- and interinstitutional comparisons about how much community college faculty teach and the cost of that instruction at the discipline level.

Benchmarking Instructional Costs and Productivity: The Kansas Study

K. Patricia Sumner, Regina G. Brewer

Institutions of higher education face increased pressure to contain costs and manage human and fiscal resources more effectively and efficiently. In 1998, Congress created a National Commission on the Cost of Higher Education and asked it to develop recommendations that would guide and inform public policy with respect to cost containment. Among the commission's recommendations was a call for "individual institutions, acting with technical support from appropriate higher education associations, [to] conduct efficiency self-reviews to identify effective cost-saving steps that are relevant to institutional mission and quality improvement. Academic leaders should communicate the results of these self-reviews widely, providing the campus community and institutional constituents with information on issues such as . . . faculty teaching loads, average class size, faculty and student ratios" (Drotning, 1998, p. 2).

In addition, in July 2005, as part of the reauthorization of the Higher Education Act, the House Education Committee passed a bill that would require institutions to report their tuition and fees each year and pay a fee if their costs exceeded an indexed limit. The legislation also called for the creation of a "college consumer profile" for each institution. Among the items to be included in the profile were instructional expenditures per full-time-equivalent student and the percentages of full- and part-time faculty. While this legislation has not yet become law, it illustrates the accountability community colleges and other institutions of higher education are increasingly facing.

NEW DIRECTIONS FOR COMMUNITY COLLEGES, no. 134, Summer 2006   © Wiley Periodicals, Inc.
Published online in Wiley InterScience (www.interscience.wiley.com) • DOI: 10.1002/cc.232

Because it is not likely that there will be a massive infusion of additional resources into community colleges, new programs and initiatives will have to be funded largely through resource reallocation strategies. And if community colleges are to preserve broad access to higher education, tuition increases must be limited and replaced by managerial practices that encourage cost containment and enhanced productivity. Thus there is a great need for data on instructional costs and productivity in community colleges.

Although there is a sophisticated data-sharing consortium that provides national benchmark data on instructional costs and faculty workloads to more than four hundred four-year colleges and universities (Middaugh, 2001), it cannot be used at the two-year college level due to the fundamental differences in faculty work across the two sectors of higher education. Specifically, community college faculty are not expected to conduct scholarly research, and there are many more part-time instructors in community colleges than in four-year institutions. Indeed, in many two-year colleges, adjuncts teach more than half of all course offerings. Therefore, administrators in the Johnson County Community College Office of Institutional Research (JCCC OIR) developed a model, called the Kansas Study of Institutional Costs and Productivity, that collects and disseminates data on community college instructional costs and faculty productivity. The purpose of the project is to create a national database that is accessible to any community college willing to share information on their instructional costs and productivity.

Kansas Study History

In 2002, the JCCC OIR applied for and was awarded a three-year, $282,000 grant from the U.S. Department of Education Fund for the Improvement of Postsecondary Education (FIPSE) to examine instructional costs and productivity in community colleges by academic discipline. A twenty-one-member advisory committee, composed of representatives from community colleges and national higher education associations, was created to provide input and guidance on the study's scope, methodology, definitions, and design. With knowledge gained from the four-year model, the advisory committee designed a community college data collection instrument, conducted two pilot studies, and analyzed the data. Based on the pilot study results, the committee finalized the data collection instrument, data definitions, and instructions, and modified results tables for clarity and ease of understanding. In January 2004 the Kansas Study entered into its first year of implementation.

Data Collection Instrument

Community colleges wishing to participate in the Kansas Study complete an enrollment form and designate a contact person at their institution who will be responsible for data entry. For most institutions, this is the director of institutional research or an analyst in that office. Upon receipt of the enrollment form, the contact person is e-mailed an institutional demographic profile template, an Excel data entry template, data entry instructions, a glossary, and a list of academic disciplines and associated Kansas Study codes.

The demographic profile template provides information on an institution's size (enrollments of fewer than 5,000 students, 5,000 to 9,999, and 10,000 and above), location (urban, suburban, or rural), and campus type (single campus, multicampus college, or multicollege district). These criteria can be used in the project's peer analysis tool described later in this chapter.

The Kansas Study collects information on instructional activities and costs at the academic discipline level. Only data on courses eligible for Title IV funding are included in the analysis. The academic discipline, often corresponding to a department within the institution, is defined by a Kansas Study code based loosely on the Classification of Instructional Programs code associated with that discipline. Data are reported as a function of the instructional unit and not as a function of the departmental or organizational source from which the instructor's salary is paid. For instructors who teach in two different disciplines (for example, history and philosophy), but whose salary is paid by only one of the disciplines, student credit hours are reported under both disciplines and the instructional salary data are prorated to each discipline based on the number of student credit hours generated in that department. This methodology differs substantially from that used to examine institutional costs and faculty productivity at four-year institutions, as budget units are organized differently in two- and four-year colleges. The Kansas Study advisory committee feels this methodology better reflects the actual community college instructional workload and costs for any given academic discipline.

The data collection instrument is divided into two parts: instructional workload and instructional costs. The instructional workload section examines faculty type and student credit hours taught in a fall term for each reported academic discipline. Data are reported for three groups of faculty: full-time faculty, adjunct or part-time faculty, and "other full-time employees," which includes administrative and professional personnel at the institution who teach but whose primary job responsibility is administrative. Data for full-time faculty members who are teaching additional courses over and above their contracted load and who receive a supplemental or overload contract are reported as full-time. Institutions identify a full-time equivalency (FTE) for each of the faculty types within a discipline. The student credit hours generated by each of the faculty types are determined and reported. Benchmarks are created on the percent of student credit hours taught by faculty type. Using an instructional FTE for faculty provides for an accurate teaching-load benchmark and enables institutions to make comparisons to a national benchmark and to comparable institutions. Participants are able to answer such questions as whether teaching patterns at their institution are similar to or different from those in their selected peer groups. Results include the percent of credit hours taught by faculty type and number of student credit hours taught per FTE faculty type. For example, results may show the proportion of student credit hours for English that are taught by full- and part-time faculty or might compare the number of student credit hours taught per FTE full-time faculty compared to the number taught per FTE part-time faculty.

The Kansas Study instrument also collects data on instructional costs. For each reported academic discipline, institutions provide total student credit hours for a fiscal or academic year, as well as all associated faculty salaries and benefits. The template also asks for cost data for department chairs and support staff, such as department administrative assistants and tutors. Cost data for disciplines that have dedicated labs (for example, math labs) are included in this section as well. Results reported for this section are thus direct costs per student credit hour attributable to a specific discipline.

Participating community colleges may choose to participate in either the instructional workload or instructional cost portions of the survey, or both. Institutions are asked to provide data for a minimum of ten academic disciplines, but may provide data for as many as they wish. However, only disciplines for which five or more institutions provide data are included in benchmark calculations and project reports. Data are reported as national refined means (that is, without data that fall outside two standard deviations from the overall mean).

Depending on the number of academic disciplines a community college reports and the accuracy of their data, the initial data collection process can be lengthy. While instructional workload data are usually available to an institution, instructional cost data are not always easily available at the discipline level in community colleges. Also, since cost data follow the discipline(s) in which the instructor teaches and not necessarily the source of the instructor's salary, it takes time to allocate salaries and benefits for those faculty teaching in more than one discipline or being paid by one discipline but generating student credit hours in another. In addition, some community colleges use central rather than departmental budgeting. For such institutions, faculty salaries and benefits are prorated based on student credit hours generated for a given discipline. Once an institution has developed a methodology for collecting and reporting cost data, the reporting burden in future years is greatly reduced.

Kansas Study Web Site

During the first year of the Kansas Study, a Web development firm designed the Kansas Study Web site (www.kansasstudy.org). The public section of the site provides general information about the study, including a history of the project, a list of academic disciplines, a sample of the data template, and an example of the result tables. There is also a "participants only" section at which, with a username and password, community colleges participating in the Kansas Study are able to access national means tables, obtain their own institutional reports, and use the peer analysis tool, which allows them to compare their own institutional data with those from peer institutions by academic disciplines. Since January 2005, all community colleges have been able to enter data directly into the "participants only" section rather than to a separate Excel workbook.

Kansas Study Results

Results of the first two Kansas Study data collection and reporting cycles produced a set of community college benchmarks that administrators can use to learn more about faculty workload, productivity, and instructional costs by academic discipline. These benchmarks, when used in conjunction with institutional data, offer an institution a fuller understanding of how it is using its resources. Sixty-nine institutions from twenty-five states participated in the 2005 iteration of the Kansas Study. Twenty-six were urban institutions, twenty-four suburban, and nineteen rural. Twenty-nine institutions enrolled fewer than 5,000 students, another twenty enrolled between 5,000 and 9,999, and twenty more enrolled more than 10,000 students. Thirty of the participating institutions were single-campus colleges; thirty-seven were multicampus institutions. As well, two multicollege districts participated in the 2005 Kansas Study.

Participation in the Kansas Study is on a voluntary basis. Because the population for the study is self-selecting, it is not a random sample, and results from the study cannot be generalized to a larger population of community colleges and academic disciplines. Further, data only reflect direct instructional expenditures on salary and benefits for faculty and support staff and do not constitute a full cost model for community colleges. Nevertheless, the results of the study are useful for participating community colleges. Administrators can use results as part of an instructional program review process, in assessing their program in comparison to peers, and as a tool for considering whether or not to increase or reduce faculty workload or the number of positions within a discipline. The state of Tennessee, for example, has incorporated Kansas Study data into its performance funding model, which allows comparison of results not only within the state but also with peer institutions across the nation.

Benchmarking data are provided to participating institutions through a series of national norms tables. These tables present data only for those academic disciplines for which data were reported by five or more institutions. The 2005 study reported data on ninety-nine academic disciplines. The most frequently submitted disciplines were mathematics (excluding developmental mathematics), biological and life sciences, psychology, computer and information sciences, and business administration and management.

Results are reported in three sets of data in Table 1.1. The first set provides information on the proportion of student credit hours taught by full- or part-time faculty. For example, in fall 2002, the average proportion of student credit hours taught by full-time faculty for accounting was 72 percent. The second set uses data from the instructional workload section and reports student credit hours taught per FTE faculty as well as FTE students per FTE faculty. The third set uses data from the instructional cost section of the data collection template and provides ratios on instructional costs per student credit hour. The overall national ratios tend to show that general education courses such as history, math, and psychology have low costs per student credit hour, while career programs in allied health, such as nursing and occupational therapy, tend to have higher instructional costs.

While the national reports provide data for all disciplines, the institutional reports are customized for each individual institution. Kansas Study participants receive three institutional reports that mirror the national norms tables and compare their institution's data to those national norms. These tables only present data for academic disciplines for which data were reported by five or more institutions. The first institutional report compares the percent of student credit hours taught by faculty type for the participating institution with the national refined mean. The second report provides comparisons of the average student credit hours taught by FTE faculty type, as reported by the participating institution, with the national refined mean. The third institutional report illustrates the instructional costs per student credit hour for the participating institution, along with the national refined mean. Institutional data are also available in an Excel format that can be easily downloaded for internal reporting.

In addition to comparing institutional data to national norms, participating community colleges may use the peer analysis tool to create custom peer groups for benchmarking purposes. Peer institutions may be selected by name from a dropdown list of participating institutions or by specific demographic criteria, including institutional location, size, and type. In order to maintain participant confidentiality, participating institutions must select a minimum of seven peer institutions with which to benchmark.

After peer institutions have been selected, participants are prompted to select a reporting period and one of three available report tables: Percent of Student Credit Hours Taught by Faculty Type, Student Credit Hours Taught and FTE Students per FTE Faculty, and Instructional Costs per Student Credit Hour. Finally, participants are prompted to select the academic discipline(s) they wish to benchmark. They may select as many disciplines as they wish.

After all required selections have been made, a report table is generated. To ensure confidentiality, only the local institution is identified on the table; selected peer institutions are identified only by randomly assigned letters. While the requesting institution knows which seven or more institutions are included in the peer group, data identities are masked so that it

Table 1.1. The Kansas Study 2003–04: National Refined Means

Academic Discipline	Percent Student Credit Hours Taught by:			Student Credit Hours Taught per Total FTE	FTE Students per Total FTE Faculty	Instructional Costs per Student Credit Hour
	Full-Time Faculty	Part-Time Faculty	Full-Time Employees			
Biological Sciences	66	33	0	347	23	$66.00
Business Administration	62	35	1	273	18	$76.00
Mathematics	70	28	1	325	22	$70.00
Nursing	87	12	0	268	18	$210.00
Psychology	55	43	2	406	27	$47.00

is impossible to associate responses with specific institutions. The peer comparison results may be downloaded to Excel for further analysis.

Participation in both sections of the data collection process, while not required, assists administrators in better understanding the data. For example, institutions at which costs for an individual discipline are much higher than at peer institutions can look at the instructional activities of their faculty compared to those of their peers. Perhaps one institution hires fewer part-time faculty, or maybe a college's full-time faculty generate fewer student credit hours than their peers at other institutions.

While the Kansas Study does not adjust for differences in economic costs across the country, community college administrators should consider this factor in selecting peer institutions. For example, community colleges on either the East or the West Coast may not want to compare instructional costs with colleges in the Midwest, as the cost of living—and thus instructional expenditures—is much lower in the middle of the country.

Kansas Study in the Future

Because the Kansas Study is funded by a FIPSE grant, institutional participation is currently free of charge and, as a result of a one-year no-cost extension from FIPSE, will remain so in the 2006 data collection and reporting cycle. However, in 2007 and following years an institutional subscription fee will be necessary to support continuation of the project. The 2006 Kansas Study data collection cycle opened for enrollment in February 2006; data are due by July. National and institutional reports, as well as the "participant only" section of the Web site, will open for peer selection and benchmarking in fall 2006.

Community colleges are encouraged to participate in the Kansas Study every year in order to develop trend data that can answer why, over time, a discipline's metrics are similar to or different from either the national norms or those of peer institutions. While some institutions have developed homegrown cost analyses, participation in the Kansas Study enables community colleges to obtain national and peer comparisons with common definitions. The Kansas Study is unique in that comparisons are at the academic discipline level—rather than institution level—instructional workloads are by faculty type, and there are common data definitions and methodology.

The major benefit of participating in the Kansas Study, however, lies in the ability to select comparable institutions that reflect a community college's primary peer group or those of similar size, location, and campus type. Peer analysis allows an institution to assess instructional costs in comparison to those at similar institutions, and national discipline benchmarks allow administrators to make better-informed decisions about resource allocation and utilization.

As more and more states enact legislation or regulations mandating faculty accountability and instructional cost reporting, the Kansas Study will continue to provide a credible national benchmarking tool for community colleges. Tennessee, for example, has mandated use of Kansas Study data for all thirteen state-supported community colleges as part of the state's performance funding model (see Chapter Two for more information about how Tennessee community colleges use data from the Kansas Study).

References

Drotning, L. *College Costs and Prices: Report of the National Commission on the Cost of Higher Education.* AIR Alert #8. Tallahassee, Fla.: Association for Institutional Research, 1998. http://airweb.org/page.asp?page=114. Accessed Feb. 12, 2006.

Middaugh, M. F. *Understanding Faculty Productivity: Standards and Benchmarks for Colleges and Universities.* San Francisco: Jossey-Bass, 2001.

K. *PATRICIA SUMNER is information analyst in the Office of Institutional Research at Johnson County Community College (Kansas).*

REGINA G. BREWER is market and survey research analyst in the Office of Institutional Research at Johnson County Community College (Kansas).

2

This chapter describes how the Kansas Study of Community College Instructional Costs and Productivity can be used in state, institutional, and regional accreditation contexts.

Uses of Kansas Study Data at State System and Institutional Levels

George E. Malo, Ellen J. Weed

The Kansas Study of Instructional Costs and Productivity provides comparative data important to accountability processes and decision making at both state system and institutional levels. This chapter discusses the ways in which a public higher education governing board and one of its community colleges have used Kansas Study data in program review, system and state policymaking, planning and accreditation, assessment, institutional management, and other accountability processes. While comparative data are invaluable to institutions of higher education, and community colleges in particular, benchmarking information must be used appropriately, especially in a public arena. We hope that this chapter will also provide insight on appropriate uses of Kansas Study data.

Kansas Study Data from a System Perspective

The Tennessee Board of Regents is among the largest public systems of higher education in the country. In fall 2005, more than 185,000 students were enrolled in its six universities, thirteen community colleges, and twenty-six technology centers. The community colleges enroll 75,000 students and range in size from 2,500 to 12,000 students. The Kansas Study provides an opportunity for a system of this size to address accountability issues in a manner that is manageable and consistent across the system. All thirteen of the public community colleges in Tennessee participate in the Kansas Study.

NEW DIRECTIONS FOR COMMUNITY COLLEGES, no. 134, Summer 2006 © Wiley Periodicals, Inc.
Published online in Wiley InterScience (www.interscience.wiley.com) • DOI: 10.1002/cc.233

About the time that the Kansas Study was being formulated, the Tennessee Board of Regents (TBR) undertook an accountability initiative called Defining Our Future. One element of this initiative addressed the need for specific information on program costs and faculty workload. Although all TBR institutions were participating in a statewide cost model that provided program costs and information on faculty workload, the model did not allow for the national benchmarks called for in the Defining Our Future initiative. By participating in the Kansas Study, the TBR system was able to obtain much-needed national benchmarks for its community colleges while still determining program costs and faculty workload information. As a result, the TBR decided to replace the statewide cost model with the Kansas Study and the similar Delaware Study (for use in four-year universities). Indeed, the TBR was so convinced of the importance of the Kansas Study to the system and its institutions that it wrote a computer program to help campuses obtain the necessary data elements. This program enables the thirteen community colleges to submit Kansas Study information in a way that is consistent across campuses without overtaxing each college's small institutional research staff.

Appropriate Uses of Kansas Study Data. Information from the Kansas Study enables the TBR system and its institutions to make informed policy and management decisions. For example, faculty workload data provide information useful for examining staffing patterns and needs. When data are compared to those from peer institutions, one can assess whether current workloads or class sizes within a discipline are reasonable or need to be addressed. However, one concern expressed by both board members and campus administrators was potential misuse of the data. With the former statewide cost study, many policymakers requested comparisons among institutions. Because several factors, such as diversity in size and programming among institutions, were not taken into account, comparisons were inappropriate and often misinterpreted. Depending on a variety of factors, including the diversity of community colleges within a system, it may not be appropriate to use Kansas Study data to compare institutions within the system, but rather as a tool for intra-institutional decision making. The data can help assess the adequacy of various accountability initiatives, assist campuses with program management, inform cost analyses, provide benchmarks for use in strategic planning and performance, and provide documentation for accreditation. For example, institutions can compare the percentage of adjuncts teaching in a discipline with that at peer institutions and use that information for making decisions about their staffing patterns. Examples of how Nashville State Technical Community College uses Kansas Study data for accreditation and institutional decision making are presented later in this chapter.

In order to ensure the appropriate use of cost-model data among its community colleges, the TBR system formed an ad hoc committee of chief academic officers, institutional researchers, and system central office staff. This committee was charged with recommending parameters for the use of

Kansas Study information, adopting key indicators for framing instructional productivity and effectiveness reporting, instituting a peer selection process, and developing common questions to assist institutions in providing data used in evaluation and decision making. The committee also articulated a number of recommendations to help campuses avoid misusing Kansas Study data. First, the information should be used as a tool for institutional decision making about resource allocation, program review, and strategic and operational planning. Second, the most appropriate way an institution can use the data is to support informed decision making. The key indicators described later in this chapter provide a framework for analyzing these data in order to demonstrate institutional effectiveness. Third, the data must be analyzed, at a minimum, in three-year trends. The data are not intended for drawing conclusions based on a single point in time. Using trend data will help to ensure that unreasonable conclusions are not drawn from what may be an anomaly. Finally, the data should be used to inform a specific department or discipline, not the institution as a whole. In many cases, the data cannot be aggregated to draw conclusions about or to generate a profile of the entire institution. Peer comparisons are best made at the discipline or department level.

The ad hoc committee also recommended the adoption of three key indicators for using Kansas Study data. These indicators are standard for all TBR institutions and form the central dataset from which the TBR system analyses are derived. Although the Kansas Study reports produce a multitude of indicators, the committee identified those that are the most useful to the system, its institutions, and policymakers. Individual institutions can add other indicators for internal management purposes, and many community colleges do so. The committee recommended the following indicators:

Full-Time Equivalent (FTE) Students Taught by FTE Instructional Staff by Discipline. The committee considered this indicator to be important because it provides a perspective on faculty workload. The committee members also suggested that reporting FTE by discipline would encourage workload analysis at the department level, rather than focusing on individual faculty members.

Student Credit Hours by FTE Faculty as a Percentage of National Norm by Discipline. The committee endorsed "percentage of" rather than "percentage difference from" as TBR's standard indicator. Community colleges may still analyze the data differently for internal use. Since the TBR system was seeking a benchmark for examining comparative staffing patterns and faculty workload across programs, the committee also considered this indicator to be important.

Percentage of Student Credit Hours Taught by Full-Time Faculty (Including Department or Discipline Heads). The TBR system office and community colleges are often asked by policymakers, students, and parents about the number of courses taught by full-time faculty. The committee members believed this indicator is important to answer those questions. The indicator will also provide the full-time faculty and adjunct ratios necessary for accreditation and staffing pattern reviews.

Because there are many ways of determining comparison groups, the ad hoc committee also recommended a standard methodology for peer selection so that there is face validity in institutional accountability reporting. Currently, all TBR institutions have a peer set as defined by the Tennessee Higher Education Commission. Since these peers are institutional and not discipline-specific, the committee recommended that a different set of peers be established according to three standards, two of which apply to community colleges. First, for system reporting, all institutions report data by discipline and by highest degree offered. Since the Kansas Study reports by discipline, the committee recommended that the peers be selected by discipline. Second, for institutional use only, each discipline may select peer groups within the guidelines established by that institution. Since programs are different across disciplines, the committee believed that institutions should tailor their peers by each discipline in order for the Kansas Study data to be most meaningful and useful.

The TBR and its institutions must be accountable to the public for the quality and cost of programs and services delivered. With the former Tennessee cost model, administrators and legislators tended to compare program costs across institutions, formulating their own inferences about the effectiveness and efficiencies of programs. Now the board has the opportunity to report accountability data to the public by focusing on benchmarking, change, and results. In other words, the board can report how campuses are seeking improvements by addressing instructional costs and program efficiencies, which is especially important at a time when budget reductions and tuition increases are prevalent. With this reporting in mind, the committee recommended that the TBR system adopt key questions to guide institutions in analyzing their own Kansas Study data. These questions lead a community college to evaluate its institutional effectiveness and efficiency by formulating a strategy that provides a rationale or justification for their decisions based on data. This case-making strategy is consistent with the accreditation requirements of the Southern Association of Colleges and Schools, the accrediting agency for Tennessee colleges and universities. As a result, Tennessee community colleges can now report accountability data in a more proactive, rather than reactive, manner.

Analysis of data over the past two years was guided by three key indicators. First, the ratio of FTE students per FTE instructors, which is a proxy for class size, was assessed by discipline and across institutional peers. Second, student credit hours per FTE faculty was assessed as a percentage of the national norm by discipline. Third, the percentage of student credit hours taught by full-time faculty was assessed by discipline and across peer institutions. The results of these assessments provided data for community colleges to determine if they believed changes or improvements were necessary. If so, institutions provided rationales for making these changes or improvements and discussed the factors that may have contributed to differences.

Although analyzing these three key indicators is critical, using the information to make responsible decisions or improve practice is much more valuable to the general public than simply reporting information. Thus, we asked community colleges the following questions, from which an institution, the system, and the general public can derive value. First, can the institution provide a rationale, from its analysis of the allocation of faculty, that it is moving toward improvement in efficiency? In other words, can the institution provide evidence that it is achieving a desired level of instructional efficiencies and outcomes through faculty-allocation decisions? Second, in comparison to peer institutions, can the community college show that it is effectively using its faculty as a resource to address the system's priorities and fulfill its distinctive mission? Third, can the institution provide evidence that it is improving its contributions to the state's needs and institutional priorities, and do these contributions reflect a responsible use of resources that meets or exceeds those of its peers?

Using Kansas Study Data in Strategic Planning. The Tennessee Board of Regents believes that the benchmarks provided by the Kansas Study are important to a community college's strategic plan. TBR institutions have developed their 2005–10 strategic plans around four priority areas: leadership, access, quality, and resourcefulness. As part of the quality priority, community colleges are to provide evidence of program quality, service excellence, and the value of its general education program to students and the community. The board has requested that each community college incorporate data from the Kansas Study into its strategic plan as evidence of improvement in management and productivity. Similarly, the community colleges are to show evidence of resourcefulness through analysis of Kansas Study data.

Using Kansas Study Data in Performance Funding. The Tennessee Board of Regents was instrumental in promoting the use of Kansas Study benchmarks and data in the state's performance funding program. Established in 1979, this performance-based incentive program rewards public colleges and universities financially for successful performance on selected student outcomes and related academic and institutional assessments. Its ultimate goal is to promote the provision of the highest quality education to students enrolled in higher education throughout the state, and its current assessment, criteria, and scoring protocols include pilot projects that can help institutions improve efficiency or effectiveness. In the past, these pilot projects have allowed Tennessee institutions the flexibility to explore various assessment initiatives.

For the 2005–10 performance funding cycle, one of eleven standards that Tennessee institutions have to meet to earn performance funding is devoted exclusively to the collection and use of Kansas Study data. Community colleges that participate each year in the data collection and reporting of the three indicators discussed in this chapter are awarded five out of one hundred possible points in performance funding. The colleges are also to submit a report providing evidence of how they used Kansas Study data in institutional planning and improvement. Although the amount is not large, and the dollar amounts vary by the institutional budgets, in some cases participation in this standard can result in funding increases approaching $70,000. The Tennessee Board of Regents linked participation in the Kansas Study to performance funding so that community colleges would gather and analyze information that can lead to institutional improvement, one of the goals of the performance funding program.

Kansas Study Data from an Institutional Perspective

Nashville State Technical Community College (NSTCC) is an urban institution that enrolls roughly seven thousand students. Between 1970 and 2002 the college only conferred associate of applied science degrees in career and technical areas. Since becoming a comprehensive community college in 2002, however, enrollment patterns have changed significantly, making it especially important to use data to identify campus trends and make comparisons with peer institutions.

Nashville State participated in the Kansas Study during its initial implementation year (2004). Even during that first year, the Kansas Study provided rich information about the efficiency and cost of academic programs. The college has begun to integrate Kansas Study data into assessment and decision-making processes, though all parties agree that major decisions must be based on a minimum of three-year trends. However, the first year's Kansas Study data were useful for examining comparative staffing patterns and faculty workloads across programs and institutions. These data are now included in college program reviews, accreditation reports, and academic audits. This section describes the specific ways in which NSTCC has used Kansas Study data in making both collegewide and program-level assessments and decisions. The three key Kansas Study indicators used at every level of analysis are the percent of credit hours taught by full- and part-time faculty; the number of FTE students per FTE faculty, which serves as a proxy for faculty workload and class size; and direct instructional costs per student credit hour.

At NSTCC, as on most community college campuses, there is significant variation among programs on each of these three indicators. These variations result in comparisons that are sometimes, but not always, reasonable. Because it permits comparisons of similar programs across peer institutions, the Kansas Study provides a more comprehensive basis for deciding what information makes sense and what may be problematic. For example, we were concerned that the developmental math department at NSTCC uses a higher percentage of adjunct instructors (34 percent) than does the college-level math department (19 percent). This gap suggests the existence of a campus staffing problem, possibly based on faculty expertise or course preferences. However, comparison with Kansas Study national norms revealed that, nationwide, 54 percent of developmental math and 32 percent of college-level math instructors are adjuncts. These comparisons offer reas-

NEW DIRECTIONS FOR COMMUNITY COLLEGES • DOI: 10.1002/cc

surance that while the staffing problem at NSTCC may be real, it is not unique among community colleges.

Using Kansas Study Data at the Campus Level. In fall terms for 2004 and 2005, all NSTCC department chairs received a summary table of Kansas Study data. The table included, for every program, the student credit hour production (SCH), five-year SCH trends, percent of courses taught by adjuncts for NSTCC and Kansas Study peers, student-to-faculty ratios for NSTCC and Kansas Study peers, and cost per SCH for NSTCC and Kansas Study peers. This simple-to-construct table provides a wealth of information for making decisions. The data, for example, enabled us to target our automotive services program for closer examination because costs per credit hour were the highest among Kansas Study participants. Kansas Study data were also instrumental in deciding to shift a vacant faculty position from the information systems department, where the percentage of adjuncts (27 percent) was well below the Kansas Study median of 43 percent, to visual communications, where the percentage of adjuncts (66 percent) exceeded the 55 percent Kansas Study median. In addition, the Kansas Study student-to-faculty ratio of twenty-three in biology, compared to eighteen at NSTCC, resulted in the decision to increase biology lab enrollments by two students.

Nashville State gained one unexpected insight from the first year of Kansas Study data. With enrollment increasing and state funding decreasing, the percentage of our courses taught by full-time faculty is declining. Kansas Study data revealed, however, that 89 percent of NSTCC programs were above the national median in credit hours taught by full-time faculty, and that 67 percent of NSTCC programs enjoyed lower student-to-faculty ratios than the national norms. The NSTCC percentages of adjunct and student-to-faculty ratios are encouraging and have helped boost faculty morale.

Using Kansas Study Data at the Program Level. All NSTCC programs must complete either a program review or an academic audit at least once every five years, and Kansas Study information has been added as a data requirement to these assessments. Recommendations coming out of the program reviews or audits form the basis for budget and faculty requests, major equipment requests, and help set strategic planning objectives. The Kansas Study strengthens both the rigor and the credibility of program reviews by providing national peer comparisons on faculty staffing, workloads, and instructional costs at the program level. Comparing these key indicators across selected peer programs is particularly valuable.

In particular, NSTCC has found that participation in the Kansas Study adds to the program review process by providing a national context for examining local data. For example, the computer accounting department at NSTCC experienced a 40 percent drop in SCH enrollment due to a mandated reduction in graduation requirements. This decline in total SCH production resulted in a reduction of adjunct staffing to 6 percent of courses.

The psychology department, on the other hand, grew by 72 percent over the same period, resulting in adjuncts teaching 65 percent of courses in that discipline. Comparisons with national norms enhance analyses of these two program areas in several ways. First, across the nation, 28 percent of faculty in computer accounting departments and 43 percent of instructors in psychology departments are adjuncts. Therefore, an adjunct faculty benchmark for accounting should be lower than that for psychology. Second, Kansas Study data confirm that the percentage of psychology adjuncts at NSTCC is excessive. This suggests that we need to look carefully at effectiveness indicators, because a high adjunct rate increases the workload for full-time faculty, who are responsible for developing the curriculum and advising students. Third, there is a big difference between the NSTCC psychology student-to-faculty ratio of seventeen and the national ratio of twenty-six. Simply increasing the psychology department's average class size by offering fewer classes could significantly reduce the percentage of adjuncts. It would, of course, provide students with fewer course options. Nonetheless, these figures suggest that NSTCC needs to intensively examine the number and location of psychology courses as one way to address the department's staffing problem. Fourth, Kansas Study data showed instructional costs in both the computer accounting and psychology programs to be below the national median, suggesting that total cost is not a problem at NSTCC. The high rate of adjuncts explains lower costs per student credit hour in psychology, but the computer accounting figure deserves closer study and comparison with specific peer institutions. These data help the college make decisions about programs based on staffing and productivity as well as cost. Thus, in several ways, Kansas Study data add a broader perspective and increased options to the program review process.

Using Kansas Study Data for Accreditation. NSTCC's regional accreditation agency is the Commission on Colleges of the Southern Association of Colleges and Schools (SACS). Every ten years the college submits documentation in order to comply with SACS requirements, and Kansas Study information will be used to support three core requirements. Core Requirement 2.5 requires the college to engage in ongoing planning and evaluation processes that result in continuous improvement. To comply with this requirement, NSTCC will provide analyses of all Kansas Study data by program, as well as examples of actions taken, such as assignment of a faculty position to a program with a high adjunct rate and increasing maximum class size to bring the student-to-faculty ratio up to the national median.

In order to comply with Core Requirement 2.8, NSTCC must demonstrate that it employs an adequate number of full-time faculty. Kansas Study data will allow NSTCC to compare its full-time faculty staffing by program area with that of comparable institutions and to set benchmarks for any additional faculty needs based on national data. Without Kansas Study data, we would be able to make comparisons only among NSTCC programs. This

NEW DIRECTIONS FOR COMMUNITY COLLEGES • DOI: 10.1002/cc

can be very misleading, as demonstrated by the preceding discussion of NSTCC's computer accounting and psychology departments.

SACS Core Requirement 2.11 requires demonstration of a sound financial base and financial stability. Comparing NSTCC costs per student credit hour with national data will document that the college is expending adequate resources on each program. In programs where NSTCC costs are lower (for example, horticulture) or higher (as for civil engineering technology) than national figures, detailed national data, explanations, and any plans for adjustment can be based on Kansas Study data. This type of detailed information helps convince accrediting committees that the college knows what it is doing and is a careful steward of public resources.

Kansas Study data will become increasingly useful for planning and setting campus priorities as additional institutions and years of data are included in the dataset. For example, we will be able to compare the cost and student-to-faculty ratios of our nascent English as a Second Language program with such programs in urban areas of similar size. At this point, Kansas Study data from 2005 show that, while NSTCC has a higher percentage of full-time faculty teaching ESL courses than the national norms, the cost and student-to-faculty ratios closely approximate the national median. This is very encouraging for a program with 28 percent enrollment growth between 2004 and 2005. We will continue to monitor these indicators annually. In addition, NSTCC is developing a proposal for an associate degree program in paralegal studies. The Kansas Study dataset includes nineteen institutions with similar programs. The costs, student-to-faculty ratios, and full-time faculty percentages of those nineteen institutions will provide benchmarks for projecting the costs and staffing needs of our proposed program.

Conclusion

The number of ways in which NSTCC and the Tennessee Board of Regents can use Kansas Study data will grow as the years of available data and the number of institutions participating in the project increase. Increasing the number of participants is especially important, as it will enhance the selection of appropriate peer groups at the program level and will ensure more representative national norms. Kansas Study data have been an important element in policymaking, strategic planning, performance assessment, program review, and departmental management at both the system and institutional levels. The availability of national benchmarks has already enriched the assessment process at campuses and throughout the state and will continue to do so. As well, the Kansas Study can help show the Tennessee legislature and other policymakers that public higher education in the state is accountable to the public. Providing evidence of the changes and improvements that have occurred as a result of the Kansas Study will help convince the public of the value and accountability of Tennessee's community colleges.

GEORGE E. MALO is associate vice chancellor for research and assessment at the Tennessee Board of Regents.

ELLEN J. WEED is vice president for academic affairs at Nashville State Technical Community College.

This chapter describes the content and implementation of the Noel-Levitz Student Satisfaction Inventory and explains its importance and utility for community colleges.

Assessing Expectations and Perceptions of the Campus Experience: The Noel-Levitz Student Satisfaction Inventory

Julie L. Bryant

Institutions of higher education are accountable for their performance to their trustees, state boards, accreditation agencies, employees, parents, and of course, their students. College costs are rising at a pace that is much greater than the rate of inflation, which raises expectations in the process. Student populations are becoming increasingly diverse in terms of ethnic identity, levels of academic preparedness, and reasons for attending college. Colleges face growing demands for access, affordability, and accountability, even as they confront charges of inefficiency and waste (Schroeder, 2005). With public accountability comes the expectation for increased efficiency. Student satisfaction survey results are a key way to demonstrate how a college is performing and thus contribute to overall documentation of institutional effectiveness. Research suggests that low satisfaction levels contribute to student attrition. Attrition, in turn, lowers enrollment, hinders institutional reputation, and reduces institutional vitality (Miller, 2003).

The author wishes to thank Richard Miller, research consultant at Noel-Levitz, for his contributions to this chapter.

Satisfaction Assessment and Student Retention

Satisfaction assessment—and more particularly, the campus improvements that stem from it—have been linked to several key measures of student and institutional success. Colleges and universities with higher satisfaction levels also enjoy higher retention and graduation rates, lower loan default rates, and increased alumni giving (Miller, 2003). Bailey, Bauman, and Lata (1998) identified significant differences in student satisfaction between students who persist from semester to semester and those who do not, and Bruning (2002) has demonstrated that student attitudes about the student-college relationship significantly influence student retention.

Satisfaction Measurement Methodology and the Student Satisfaction Survey Instrument

To improve the quality of student life and learning, colleges work to engage their students in the classroom and in activities outside of the classroom. But how can they be engaged if colleges do not know what students want, what they expect, or what they need? By measuring the perceptions of their student body with a satisfaction assessment survey, community colleges can identify areas in which they are performing well and areas where there is room for improvement. Satisfaction assessment is enhanced by asking students how important those same areas are to them. The level of importance, or expectation, provides an added perspective that allows colleges to view how satisfied students are within the context of what truly matters to them.

The Student Satisfaction Inventory (SSI), available from Noel-Levitz (www.noellevitz.com), asks students to review a list of expectations about their college experience. Students first indicate how important each item is to them and then rate their level of satisfaction using a seven-point Likert-type scale (where 7 = very important or very satisfied and 1 = not important or not satisfied at all). The SSI reports include an average importance score and an average satisfaction score. In addition, a performance gap is calculated by subtracting the satisfaction score from the importance score. The larger the performance gap, the greater the discrepancy between what students expect and their level of satisfaction. The smaller the performance gap, the better the institution is doing at meeting expectations.

The SSI is available in three versions: one is specific to community, junior, and technical colleges; another is for four-year private and public institutions; and the third is designed for two-year career and private colleges. It typically takes students twenty-five to thirty minutes to complete the paper-and-pencil version of the survey. National benchmarking data for each of the items and the scales on the survey are specific to the type of institution. Student responses over three academic years comprise the national comparison group. The mean satisfaction score for the individual college is compared with the same score from the national group and statistically significant differences are highlighted. This analysis allows colleges to determine if their students are significantly more or less satisfied than students across the nation. The 2005 national comparison group for community, junior, and technical colleges included more than 248,000 students from 272 institutions. The institutions include a mix of large and small two-year public institutions from urban and rural locations. The data are not weighted. All students surveyed with the SSI during the indicated timeframe are included in the national benchmarking data. If the institution prefers, it can select specific colleges from the overall list to create a specialized peer comparison group. This group must contain a minimum of seven institutions.

For institutions that want to take satisfaction assessment beyond the student experience and expand their surveying to include campus personnel, there is a parallel instrument, the Institutional Priorities Survey (IPS). This instrument allows colleges to assess the priorities of their faculty, administration, and staff on the same issues students respond to on the SSI. Campus personnel indicate a level of importance and a level of agreement (rather than satisfaction) on statements of expectation regarding the student experience. The items are parallel in language to the items on the SSI. For example, on the SSI one statement reads, "I am able to register for classes with few conflicts." On the IPS, the statement has been changed to "Students are able to register for classes with few conflicts." More than six hundred institutions have administered the IPS since it became available in 1997; 34 percent (219) of these are two-year public institutions. National benchmarking data are also available for the item and scale results for the IPS. The 2005 national data set consisted of 12,969 campus personnel from ninety-seven institutions during the three-year time frame. The SSI and IPS should be administered at the same time on campus in order to capture a particular point in time at the institution. With the combination of data from students and campus personnel, institutional leaders gain a more complete picture of the perceptions on campus and how particular issues are viewed similarly or differently, and they can begin strategic planning efforts with a more accurate view of the entire campus.

Survey Reliability and Validity

The Student Satisfaction Inventory builds on a long tradition of consumer theory, originating with the work of Cardozo (1965). The instrument views students as consumers who have a choice about whether (and where) to invest in education. More specifically, it views students as individuals who intrinsically compare their expectations about the campus experience with their actual experiences. After concluding a pilot project and validity study of the instrument in 1993, the instrument became available in 1994. Through the spring of 2005, more than two million students at more than sixteen hundred institutions have completed the inventory. Approximately one-third of these students and colleges represent two-year community, junior, and technical colleges. Based on national enrollment figures (U.S. Department of Education, 2005), approximately one out of every ten students nationwide will complete the SSI.

The Student Satisfaction Inventory offers an advantage over locally developed instruments in that it has already been tested and proven statistically reliable. In addition, locally developed instruments do not incorporate the large amount of national benchmarking data (from more than two million responses) used by the inventory. This benchmarking allows institutions to compare their students' satisfaction levels and expectations with an external perspective. Even in the area of customization—an advantage for a locally developed instrument—the SSI accommodates individual institutions' desire to assess concerns particular to their college by allowing them to add ten unique items to the survey. Although locally developed instruments can focus on particular issues of concern at a given community college, they may overlook other issues that can be identified within the broad scope of the Student Satisfaction Inventory.

Administration of the Student Satisfaction Inventory

The SSI is typically administered in one of two ways: in the classroom or via the Web. Classroom administration allows for higher response rates and students can either complete the survey during class time (which provides the best overall representative response) or on their own time (the instrument is distributed and collected by faculty members). Typical response rates for classroom administrations are 50 to 90 percent. Web administration is a relatively new alternative that institutions may use to avoid administering the survey during class time. However, the response rates tend to be much lower (20 to 30 percent). Noel-Levitz is currently working with campuses to improve these response rates through student e-mail database management (a key for online surveying) and communication or incentive programs that encourage students to respond.

Structure of the Instrument

The version of the SSI designed for community, junior, and technical colleges has seventy standard items, each rated for importance and satisfaction by the student. Institutions can customize up to an additional ten items to capture any unique college experiences; these are also structured to have an importance and satisfaction rating. In addition, six items rated for satisfaction only are focused on the responsiveness of the institution to diverse populations (such as evening students; older, returning learners; and students of color). Nine items ask for only an importance rating, allowing students to indicate how important various factors (such as cost, financial aid, reputation, and geographic setting) were in their decision to enroll. Students are then asked to respond to three summary items: their overall level of satisfaction, whether the institution is meeting their expectations, and whether they would enroll at the institution again if they had to reconsider their enrollment decision. Finally, the survey asks for responses to thirteen standard demographic items and two campus-defined demographic items. (Note: this description is based on the original Form A of the inventory. A shorter Form B is also available with forty items rated for importance and satisfaction and a few other adjustments to the structure.)

Scales

Results from the seventy items contained in the SSI are presented using twelve scales, derived through factor analysis. (For more information on the psychometric properties of the SSI, refer to the validity study conducted by Juillerat, 1995). The community, junior, and technical college version of the inventory includes the following scales.

Academic Advising and Counseling Effectiveness (seven items). This scale assesses the comprehensiveness of a community college's academic advising program. Academic advisors and counselors are evaluated on the basis of their knowledge, competence, and personal concern for student success, as well as on their approachability.

Academic Services (seven items). The academic services scale assesses the services students use to achieve their academic goals, including the library, computer labs, tutoring, and study areas.

Admissions and Financial Aid Effectiveness (six items). This scale assesses the institution's ability to enroll students in an effective manner. The scale covers issues such as the competence and knowledge of admissions counselors and the effectiveness and availability of financial aid programs.

Campus Climate (fifteen items). The campus climate scale assesses the extent to which the community college provides experiences that promote a sense of campus pride and feelings of belonging. This scale also assesses the effectiveness of the institution's channels of communication with students.

Campus Support Services (seven items). This scale assesses the quality of the support programs and services that students use to make their educational experiences more meaningful and productive, such as career counseling and new-student orientation.

Concern for the Individual (five items). This scale assesses the community college's commitment to treating each student as an individual. Assessments of those groups who frequently deal with students on a personal level (for example, faculty, advisors, campus staff) are included.

Instructional Effectiveness (fourteen items). The instructional effectiveness scale assesses students' academic experiences, the curriculum, and the campus' overriding commitment to academic excellence. This comprehensive scale covers areas such as the effectiveness of faculty in and outside of the classroom, course content, and sufficiency of course offerings.

Registration Effectiveness (nine items). This scale assesses issues associated with registration and billing. It also measures the institution's commitment to making these processes as smooth and effective as possible.

Responsiveness to Diverse Populations (six items). This scale assesses the institution's commitment to specific groups of students enrolled at the institution, including populations traditionally underrepresented in higher education, students with disabilities, commuters, part-time students, and older, returning learners.

Safety and Security (five items). The safety and security scale assesses the institution's responsiveness to students' personal safety and security on the campus. It also measures the effectiveness of both security personnel and campus facilities.

Service Excellence (nine items). This scale assesses the perceived attitude of a community college's staff—especially front-line staff—toward students. It pinpoints the areas of the campus where quality service and personal concern for students are rated most and least favorably.

Student Centeredness (six items). This final scale assesses the campus's efforts to convey to students that they are important to the institution. This scale measures the extent to which students feel welcome and valued.

Uncovering Enrollment Factors

Although the SSI scales primarily address items related to the student experience and retention, the survey also asks students to respond to nine items regarding factors in their decision to enroll. These items provide data on academic reputation, financial aid, cost, geographic setting, size, campus appearance, recommendations from family and friends, personalized attention prior to enrollment, and the opportunity to participate in athletics—all of which influence students' decisions to enroll. Admissions and marketing personnel can use these data to position their campuses for recruiting future classes.

Multiple Ways for Colleges to Review the Data

The SSI reports provide community colleges with opportunities to review their results in multiple ways. Noel-Levitz suggests that colleges begin by reviewing the demographic results to see the number of students who completed the survey and to understand the demographic mix. This allows college leaders to determine if the survey respondents are representative of the overall student population. It is important to review the results within the context of the students represented in the sample. For example, if only daytime students are surveyed, then an institution cannot assume that the data are representative of the experiences of evening students at the college. Second, college leaders often review the scales in order of importance as determined by the scale scores. This review provides an overview of the areas or categories that matter most to students.

The top priorities for the college as identified by the responses are found in the Strategic Planning Overview segment of the results. This overview lists the strengths and challenges for the college as identified in the data set. Strengths are defined as items above the midpoint in importance and in the upper quartile of satisfaction scores—areas where the college is performing very well and is meeting or exceeding student expectations. Challenges are identified as items above the midpoint in importance and in the lower quartile of satisfaction or upper quartile of performance gaps. Challenges are the top priority for response, as they identify areas in which the college is currently failing to meet student expectations. Typical challenges at two-year public institutions include too few classes scheduled at convenient times and inadequate financial aid for most students. Colleges may respond by reviewing their course scheduling to determine if it is student-centered or faculty-centered. In the area of financial aid, colleges may explore their aid policies and whether they are accurately communicating the financial options available to students. The matrix in Figure 3.1 provides a visual guide.

The scale and item results are presented alongside the appropriate national comparison-group data so institutions can benefit from external benchmarking. The mean difference in satisfaction between the campus score and the national benchmark is calculated, along with statistical significance based on a two-tailed t test. Items with a positive mean difference indicate that students at the college are more satisfied than students in the national comparison group; items with a negative mean difference indicate that students at the college are less satisfied than students nationally. While it is important to have this external viewpoint, Noel-Levitz urges institutions to use the Strategic Planning Overview list of strengths and challenges as the primary guide for institutional action. Many factors contribute to the satisfaction levels of students in the national comparison group, including campus location, size, and student diversity. These demographic factors can contribute to typical levels of satisfaction and can influence whether students at an individual college appear to be more or less satisfied. The Strategic Planning Overview is the most accurate approach because it relies on an internal analysis of the college's own data set and uses the priorities of its own students to establish relative strengths and challenges.

Optional reporting is available to supplement the standard data analysis. Target-group reporting provides analyses segmented by specific demographic variables, such as male and female, first-year and second-year, day and evening students. Campus leaders can use this report to determine if top challenges (items of high importance and low satisfaction, as defined on the list of challenges in the Strategic Planning Overview) are consistent across various demographic groups or are unique to particular subpopulations, which may provide opportunities for targeted initiatives. Year-to-year comparison reports are available to colleges that have administered the sur-

Figure 3.1. Matrix for Prioritizing Institutional Action

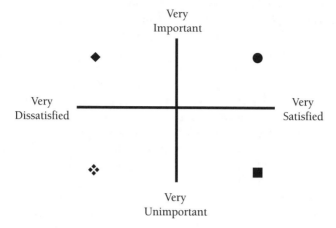

♦ High importance and low satisfaction are areas where the community college is not adequately servicing its students; these areas should be addressed immediately.

● High importance and high satisfaction are areas of institutional strength that should be highlighted in promotional materials.

❖ Low importance and low satisfaction areas are of less importance to students; community colleges should investigate why.

■ Low importance and high satisfaction are areas from which it might be beneficial to redirect institutional resources to areas of higher importance.

vey over multiple years. These reports allow community colleges to identify areas where there have been significant changes in satisfaction over time, and they provide direction to campus leaders on initiatives that are working, as well as those areas that may need further attention.

How Campuses Use Satisfaction Data

While conducting satisfaction assessment is a way to show students that the institution cares about their perceptions and their educational experience, actively responding to student-identified issues is just as important. After data have been collected, reviewed, and shared throughout the campus, college leaders should identify and promote initiatives in response to student concerns. Data on the shelf have no power; data actively used to drive decision making can have the power to improve the success of the institution.

Community colleges can use the results from the inventory to identify key challenges and prioritize initiatives for strategic planning and retention activities; establish the basis for focus group discussions leading to further, qualitative inquiry; identify key strengths for internal and external public relations efforts and recruitment activities; create a foundational element for accreditation requirements; explore the different perceptions and experiences of various subpopulations on campus; and track satisfaction assessment over time to determine where improvements have been made and identify current issues the college faces. In order to be most effective, satisfaction assessment needs to be systematic, not a "once and done" activity. Students should be surveyed, results reviewed and discussed, initiatives put in place, college faculty and staff informed of the changes made, and then students should be surveyed again. Continuously monitoring student perceptions and actively responding to them is critical for institutional and student success. Students want to be at a college that cares about them, and when the college responds with improvements in the areas that matter most, students are able to see tangible evidence that the institution cares about their experience.

Excerpts from the 2005 National Student Satisfaction and Priorities Report

Noel-Levitz produces the National Student Satisfaction and Priorities Report annually to review areas in which colleges are meeting or failing to meet student expectations. This section highlights the results for 248,307 students from 272 community, junior, and technical colleges who completed the survey between the fall of 2002 and the spring of 2005. These data are excerpted from the complete 2005 National Student Satisfaction and Priorities Report published by Noel-Levitz. The full report, published each summer, is available on the Noel-Levitz Web site.

Findings from the 2005 report reveal a general trend in priorities. Based on the responses from students nationwide, the following six SSI scales ranked as most important to students: instructional effectiveness, registration effectiveness, academic advising and counseling, concern for the individual, academic services, and admissions and financial aid. The rankings in 2005 are consistent with rankings from the past several years.

The largest gaps—areas of high importance but low satisfaction—occurred in academic advising and counseling, admissions and financial aid, and concern for the individual. This is the most effective element of the SSI as an institutional planning tool, as these gap scores point to areas that two-year institutions should make their highest priority in terms of improving student satisfaction.

The following items, listed in order of importance, have been identified as the top ten strengths by students at community, junior, and technical colleges across the nation:

NEW DIRECTIONS FOR COMMUNITY COLLEGES • DOI: 10.1002/cc

1. The quality of instruction I receive in most classes is excellent.
2. Nearly all faculty are knowledgeable in their fields.
3. There are a good variety of courses provided on this campus.
4. I am able to experience intellectual growth here.
5. The campus is safe and secure for all students.
6. Program requirements are clear and reasonable.
7. My academic advisor is approachable.
8. Faculty are usually available after class and during office hours.
9. Computer labs are adequate and accessible.
10. Policies and procedures regarding registration and course selection are clear and well publicized.

Following, listed in order of importance, are the top ten challenges as identified by students at community, junior, and technical colleges in 2005:

1. Classes are scheduled at times that are convenient for me.
2. I am able to register for classes I need with few conflicts.
3. Adequate financial aid is available for most students.
4. The amount of student parking on campus is adequate.
5. The school does what it can to help me reach my educational goals.
6. Students are notified early in the term if they are doing poorly in a class.
7. My academic advisor is knowledgeable about the transfer requirements of other schools.
8. The college shows concern for me as an individual.
9. Parking lots are well lighted and secure.
10. Faculty are understanding of students' unique life circumstances.

The following enrollment factors (why students chose their institution) are indicated in order of importance for students at community, junior, and technical colleges in 2005:

1. Cost
2. Financial aid
3. Academic reputation
4. Geographic setting
5. Personalized attention prior to enrollment
6. Size of institution
7. Campus appearance
8. Recommendations from family and friends
9. Opportunity to participate in athletics

Although national data are valuable in that they provide a broader perspective of student enrollment decisions, it is important for colleges to survey their own students to identify unique strengths, challenges, and factors in the decision to enroll. Colleges make the best-informed decisions for their own institution when the results are specific to students at that college.

Concluding Thoughts

Satisfaction assessment results are key indicators of the student experience inside and outside of the classroom. Satisfaction survey data provide important direction for campus strategic planning efforts. Institutions that measure satisfaction can systematically improve the quality of their undergraduate experience and can offer more educational value to students and families.

Campuses that systematically measure and act on measures of student satisfaction appear to enjoy the greatest levels of institutional and student success. Ultimately, community colleges that measure satisfaction should use the data to continuously improve the student experience, thereby fulfilling their roles as good stewards of families' and the public's financial resources.

References

Bailey, B. L., Bauman, C., and Lata, K. A. *Student Retention and Satisfaction: The Evolution of a Predictive Model.* Paper presented at the 38th annual AIR Forum, Minneapolis, Minn., May 1998. (ED 424 797)

Bruning, S. D. "Relationship Building as a Retention Strategy: Linking Relationship Attitudes and Satisfaction Evaluations to Behavioral Outcomes." *Public Relations Review,* 2002, 28(1), 39–48.

Cardozo, R. N. "An Experimental Study of Consumer Effort, Expectation, and Satisfaction." *Journal of Marketing Research,* 1965, 2, 244–249.

Juillerat, S. "Investigating a Two-Dimensional Approach to the Assessment of Student Satisfaction: Validation of the Student Satisfaction Inventory." Unpublished doctoral dissertation, Temple University, 1995.

Miller, R. *Student Satisfaction and Institutional Success.* Paper presented at the 43rd annual AIR Forum, Tampa, Fla., May 2003.

Schroeder, C. *How to Generate Purposeful Change on Your Campus: A Realistic Approach to Institutional Assessment.* Iowa City: Noel-Levitz, 2005.

U.S. Department of Education, National Center for Education Statistics. *Condition of Education.* Washington, D.C.: U.S. Department of Education, 2005.

JULIE L. BRYANT is senior director of retention solutions at Noel-Levitz, Inc.

This chapter describes Santa Fe Community College's use of the Noel-Levitz Student Satisfaction Inventory to guide iterative development of institutional improvements associated with student satisfaction.

Identifying What Matters to Students: Improving Satisfaction and Defining Priorities at Santa Fe Community College

Anne M. Kress

As the 1990s drew to a close, Santa Fe Community College (Florida), as well as many other community colleges, was confronting issues that would have seemed alien just a few years earlier: fierce competition, both from other public institutions and the more flexible and accommodating private ones; legitimization of online degree programs; increasing and ever more concrete demands for accountability from the public, state, and federal governments as well as other funding agencies; and compounding all the others, a growing consumer mentality from students (Levine and Cureton, 1998).

Recognizing that the ground rules for higher education were changing, Santa Fe Community College (SFCC) undertook an ambitious plan to change its culture and practices and renew its learner-centered focus. The college applied for and received a $1.75 million, five-year grant from the U.S. Department of Education's Title III-A Strengthening Institutions program. The overarching goal of the plan was to use technology to transform the delivery of education and support services to create a more flexible and responsive college.

NEW DIRECTIONS FOR COMMUNITY COLLEGES, no. 134, Summer 2006 © Wiley Periodicals, Inc.
Published online in Wiley InterScience (www.interscience.wiley.com) • DOI: 10.1002/cc.235

Importance of Student Perceptions

At an intuitive level, SFCC faculty and staff knew that any process of transformation had to begin with student input: their perceptions of and satisfaction with college programs and services. Of course, the very concept of
student satisfaction is not without controversy. Faculty and support professionals bristled at the notion of catering to what they saw as students' whims
in order to make them happy. Many saw this as the introduction of a business model that had no place in academe. However, while SFCC understood
this apprehension, the college also believed that acknowledging the importance of student satisfaction did not conflict with an emphasis on academic
excellence. Students were increasingly vocal in demanding convenience,
quality, service, and value for their tuition dollars and time spent in class
(Levine and Cureton, 1998), and the college needed to listen to their voices.
One critical measure of the college's ability to meet these demands was the
satisfaction levels of its students.

Selecting a Satisfaction Survey

The next step was to identify a tool with which to measure student satisfaction. Like most institutions, SFCC has several in-house instruments for
measuring discrete aspects of student interaction with the college. It collects
students' opinions of their classes and instructors as well as graduates'
assessments of the institution. However, these tools were narrowly targeted;
for example, student course evaluations took place after the college's course
withdrawal date and thus missed many of the students we needed to hear
from. In-house tools also did not provide an opportunity for extra-
institutional comparisons and benchmarking, which were essential for
SFCC's new goals. The college researched several proprietary survey instruments, and one stood out: the Noel-Levitz Student Satisfaction Inventory
(SSI). The survey allows students to indicate both the importance of and
their satisfaction with college services, which helps a college target priorities and allocate resources. The SSI is a validated, nationally normed instrument that provides a large database of two-year college-satisfaction records
for comparisons and benchmarking. The survey covers multiple aspects of
the college environment, from the classroom and student life to campus
infrastructure. This comprehensive approach allows SFCC to mine the
resulting data to reveal students' perceptions of critical college functions
such as advisement, registration, and instruction. Because the SSI allows colleges to request targeted reports, SFCC can easily parse the results to identify differences across specific cohorts (for example, by full-time or part-time
students, different age groupings, or specific ethnic or racial groups). So, in
many respects, the survey offers a specialized institutional research function, providing detailed, standard reports that crystallize essential student
information for college decision makers.

Survey Methodology

Before administering the SSI, and because it would be relying on data generated from the survey to inform institutional practice, SFCC spent time thinking through its implementation methodology. The college wanted to gather unduplicated data from students at all stages of enrollment with the institution—from their first term to their last. It was important to capture as complete a picture of student perceptions as possible, so SFCC implemented the SSI approximately six weeks into the fall term, which allowed new students time to assess how the college was fulfilling their expectations while still enabling us to hear from students who might eventually drop their courses. We also wanted to capture SFCC's full diversity. Therefore, we chose to gather a purposeful, non-random sample by surveying students in English course sequences. This sampling frame was greatly influenced by two factors: SFCC's student demographics and the objectives of the Title III project that financed the SSI. The majority of SFCC students, approximately two-thirds, are in the associate of arts program with the explicit goal of university transfer upon degree completion. Workforce and career programs account for less than one-third of the college's enrollment (with non-degree-seeking students comprising the remainder). The Title III project goals addressed the retention and completion of associate of arts students, whose performance lagged behind that of their career-track peers. Many of these students begin their English coursework in developmental or English-for-academic-purposes courses, and all are required to take three sequential courses in college-level English. Thus, the sampling frame used these courses to gather representative, unduplicated responses from SFCC associate of arts students. The sample was also stratified by time of day (morning, afternoon, evening) and location to ensure a broad cross section of participants. Class time is an understandably valuable commodity, so the Title III project director met with faculty prior to survey administration to explain its purpose and met with them again after the survey to share results. She also met with student groups to explain the importance of participation. After the first year, the Title III project administrators have disseminated information to both faculty and students each fall to inform them about changes at the college that were based—at least in part—on input from the student survey results.

Survey Results

The SSI reports results on an item-by-item basis and collects related items into twelve scales: academic advising and counseling, academic services, admissions and financial aid, campus climate, campus support services, concern for the individual, instructional effectiveness, registration effectiveness, responsiveness to diverse populations, safety and security, service excellence, and student centeredness. The scale results from SFCC's first SSI in 2000 provided the college with a striking portrait of student dissatisfaction.

When compared to their peers at other community colleges, SFCC students indicated lower levels of satisfaction on every scale except academic services. For example, in 2000, SFCC students reported satisfaction with concern for the individual at 4.84, compared to a national average of 5.08 (on a seven-point scale). Their satisfaction with academic advising and counseling was 4.73, compared to 5.06 nationally. Campus climate yielded a satisfaction rating of 4.98; the national average was 5.12.

An even more telling measure could be found in the performance gaps, the difference between how students rate the importance of an item and how they rate their satisfaction with it. Because the survey asks students to assign both an importance and a satisfaction level to each item, an institution can determine how well it is meeting student expectations by subtracting the satisfaction score from the importance score (Noel-Levitz, 2003). Most of SFCC's performance gaps neared or exceeded 1.0 on a seven-point scale, and almost all the performance gaps exceeded those of other two-year colleges. Students indicated the greatest discontent with such basic and critical college functions as academic advising and counseling (1.41), admissions and financial aid (1.20), instructional effectiveness (1.13), and registration effectiveness (1.03). These results suggested that students felt SFCC did not demonstrate concern for students. The college earned its largest performance gap on safety and security (1.50), a scale strongly influenced by student dissatisfaction with parking. One could—and many did—dismiss student complaints about parking as what Levine and Cureton (1998) would call a trace effect of their consumerism: in students' minds, the college had become a variant of a shopping mall, where better parking means happier shoppers. Unfortunately, SFCC's gap on this scale was 50 percent larger than that of its comparison group, suggesting that parking was a significant and real problem for students—something that could influence their ability to attend class.

Looking at the college's 2000 SSI results, an observer might indeed have assumed that SFCC is a large urban research university, as such institutions typically exhibit low student satisfaction (Astin, 1993), and our initial SSI results resembled those provided by Noel-Levitz for four-year colleges and universities. But SFCC is a midsized suburban community college whose marketing and institutional self-image stress small class sizes, ease of student access to faculty and staff, individual attention, and concern for students' academic goals. The contrast between the college's self-image and the way students perceived it was striking.

The 2000 SSI results were shared with a cross-college steering committee convened as part of the Title III project to articulate the direction of SFCC's transformation. Steering committee members included academic, student services, technology, and faculty leaders. The committee had anticipated that students would not be entirely pleased with the college, but seeing students' dissatisfaction displayed so unequivocally in stark black-and-white bar graphs and tables was still a shock. As difficult as it was to accept and then reflect on the SSI data, it quickly and viscerally made manifest some general college observations about what students felt was lacking in areas central to their success. The steering committee was committed to the viewpoint that students' responses on these surveys reflected their lived realities at SFCC and therefore affected student enrollment, success, and completion. The results had to be taken seriously and integrated into institutional planning and priorities.

From Results to Action

Results of the 2000 SSI afforded a view of SFCC that, initially, was not flattering or even welcome but was essential to the process of institutional transformation. However, unless the college leveraged this static view into dynamic action, the results would be moot. During each of the five years that SFCC used the SSI, the Title III steering committee of college stakeholders established a specific action plan to address student concerns. The committee recognized that in surveying students, SFCC entered into an implicit promise with its students, faculty, and staff: share your concerns and college faculty and staff will listen, research, and act. Some of the elements of the college's action plans have been easy or quick fixes while others have been longer-term projects; taken together, all have significantly changed the college. The following are examples of actions taken to address the six SSI scales on which SFCC initially found the highest performance gaps.

Academic Advising and Counseling. As described in the preceding pages, SFCC students were consistently less satisfied with academic advising and counseling than their national or regional counterparts at two-year colleges. These findings raised serious concerns, and as a result the college organized focus groups of students and advisers to investigate this issue further. Results of the focus groups were surprising: students knew very little about the college's official advisement office. Most relied on friends, random college staff, or even guesswork for advisement. SFCC immediately began a promotional campaign for its advising services. However, with an adviser-to-student ratio of 1:1,100, the college realized it had to do more. Given budget limitations, it was unlikely that SFCC could ever staff its advisement center with the number of advisers required to affect this ratio significantly, and the demands of Florida's articulation agreement between community colleges and universities made it difficult to shift any advising responsibilities to faculty, who could not be expected to keep up with all the requirements and regulations. SFCC sought a solution in a college-created "high tech, high touch" advisement system, an interactive online degree audit that would guide students through the course-selection process, freeing up advisers for one-on-one work with students as needed. The ease of access provided by the new online system also allowed the college to mandate advisement before registration, something unthinkable at SFCC prior to this project.

These systems were put in place between the 2000 and 2001 runs of the SSI, and they seemed to have affected students' perceptions of the advisement process. Student satisfaction in this area increased from 4.73 to 4.83 between 2000 and 2001 and has remained fairly constant since the change in advisement strategies. This approach has also had an unexpected effect: students began to rate academic advising and counseling services as less important. Perhaps students' ability to serve themselves via online systems played a role in their perceptions of the overall importance of these services.

Admissions and Financial Aid. As with the results for advising and counseling, SFCC students reported lower satisfaction with admissions and financial aid than did their counterparts in other two-year colleges (although this scale generates a comparatively low score across the nation). While there is little that SFCC's financial aid office can do to change the size of a student's award, the college realized it could do much more to inform students of financial aid deadlines, which would affect the type of aid awarded to students and the timeliness with which it is received. Much like the advisement office, SFCC's financial aid office engaged in a promotional blitz and completely revamped its Web site to provide much more information to students. As the office moved toward online support for students, there was improvement in student satisfaction with the timeliness of award notification: from 4.44 in 2000 to 4.51 in 2003. As well, students have gradually de-emphasized the importance of individual financial aid assistance with the advent of the more comprehensive online systems; the importance rating of this scale fell from a high of 6.00 in 2000 to 5.87 in 2003.

To serve on-site students better, financial aid (like all student services offices) created a frequently asked questions (FAQ) sheet to hand out to students waiting in line to see an adviser. Because many of the students rushing to the office at the beginning of each term need answers to the same questions, the FAQ sheet provides them with these answers without their having to wait. The FAQ sheets from all offices are also collected into booklets that are given to front-line personnel so that they are able to answer basic financial aid questions—saving time for both the financial aid office and the students.

Concern for the Individual. SFCC has long prided itself on the individualized attention it offers students, so the large performance gap on this scale—as well as the comparative difference in satisfaction between SFCC and other two-year institutions—was especially surprising. Disaggregating the data on this scale proved crucial, since there was a distinct difference in satisfaction among student ethnic groups. Hispanic students were far more dissatisfied than their white and African American peers. Looking closely, the college realized that it did not offer a clearly identified office or services specifically for Hispanic students; we surmised that this might have been a major reason that Hispanic students felt that the college didn't care about them as individuals. In 2001, SFCC instituted a multicultural student center and almost overnight, satisfaction among Hispanic students improved.

NEW DIRECTIONS FOR COMMUNITY COLLEGES • DOI: 10.1002/cc

In the 2000 survey, Hispanic students reported a satisfaction level of 5.01 with the college's concern for individual students. By 2001, their satisfaction had risen to 5.13. Their perceptions of SFCC's responsiveness to diverse populations also rose dramatically, from 5.15 in 2000 to 5.31 in 2001.

Another issue identified during focus groups with students of all races was the quality of information provided by front desk personnel, many of whom are educational aides. SFCC recognized that these workers, perhaps even more than any others because of their level of engagement with students, needed better training in college policy and practice and more timely information about changes and new activities. Therefore, the college began a formal training program supplemented with information booklets (including FAQ sheets) to assist them in their work. As with many services, SFCC saw an opportunity to leverage this model and provide students with a new online information source, and it recently launched an interactive, Web-based FAQ service called "askSantaFe." By listening closely to students' concerns and acting to address them, SFCC was able to improve their satisfaction with the college's concern for the individual from 4.84 to 4.92 between 2000 and 2003.

Instructional Effectiveness. As described above, the role faculty play in student success is paramount at community colleges, so it was imperative to involve them in framing and addressing student concerns on the SSI. This approach was especially necessary at SFCC, as our students reported lower satisfaction with instructional effectiveness than their peers in comparable institutions. As a result, and as part of the Title III Project, SFCC held monthly workshops with faculty to discuss retention, stressing the importance of high expectations and corresponding support in improving student success. Data from the SSI helped to inform these workshops by offering students' perceptions of instructional issues. The Title III staff also provided faculty with additional data on SFCC students, including demographic information and qualitative feedback gathered during focus groups. Staff worked with faculty, offering to parse and mine the data as needed for departmental planning. The college's curriculum committee worked in collaboration with the project on several activities, integrated clearly defined learning outcomes into course outlines, and created a standardized syllabus format. In the end, because of the active involvement of faculty, satisfaction on the instructional effectiveness scale improved from 5.05 in 2000 to 5.15 in 2003.

Registration Effectiveness. At SFCC, course scheduling had long been a departmental affair, and there was little coordination among departments. While this was efficient for individual departments, it resulted in a course schedule in which required classes were often offered at conflicting times. As well, some general education classes required by applied sciences programs were not offered at times that would align with the program sequence. For example, a required ethics course might be offered only in the day, leaving an evening program cohort without access to the required class. Overall, evening students were quite limited in the courses they could take, and after a few terms, many students had exhausted their options. As with most other areas of student dissatisfaction, the scheduling problems resulted because of a faulty system: the college did not coordinate its scheduling efforts. Once the department chairs and directors began to work as a team, focusing both on what courses need to be offered and when the students needed access, student satisfaction improved.

In addition, the college made two other significant changes. First, it instituted an online registration system with an express feature: students can type in their desired courses, times, and sites, and the system will generate up to thirty possible schedules. Students simply select one of these schedules and their registration is complete; the days of hunting for the "perfect schedule" are over. SFCC also responded to the needs of nontraditional students by implementing "flexterms"—seven-week, fast-tracked terms that allow students to complete courses in half the time. These classes appeal to students whose schedules and responsibilities off campus do not permit them to enroll in a full-length term. Registration changes particularly affected the satisfaction of older students. The satisfaction levels of students between the ages of thirty-five and forty-four improved from 5.53 in 2000 to 5.72 in 2001. All students' satisfaction on this scale improved from 5.13 to 5.26 between 2000 and 2001 before leveling out at 5.18 in 2003. This eventual downward shift is emblematic of a trend we have seen. Initially, students respond extraordinarily favorably to changes designed to address their needs; in fact, the largest increases we have seen in student satisfaction were observed between the baseline survey in 2000 and that administered the following year. However, as institutional memory about the way things used to be fades, students come to expect the new services and no longer see them as an improvement on old practice. Thus, their satisfaction levels out and the college must continually renew its commitment to understanding students' expectations.

Safety and Security. SFCC students also reported lower satisfaction on the safety and security scale than did students in comparable two-year colleges. As discussed earlier, SFCC's performance on this scale was heavily influenced by students' concerns with parking. While dissatisfaction with parking may seem a minor inconvenience, Chickering and Kytle (1999) provide a summary of research on commuter versus residential student populations, which reiterates the long-held finding that commuter students are at greater risk for attrition simply because they must make their way to college each day. Students who consistently have difficulty parking on campus are reading what Strange and Banning (2001) describe as nonverbal messages encoded in the physical environment: the lack of parking says, simply put, "go home." And because the nonverbal supersedes the verbal, once this message is received, it is difficult to retract, which conceivably makes it impossible to convince these students to return to the college. So, after initially discounting the parking concerns manifest in the 2000 SSI results as inevitable, SFCC returned to this topic in the following years, realizing that it must address the issue. One argument against the students' concerns had been that there was sufficient parking, which was technically true. However, the overflow student lot was an unpaved field that turned into a muddy mess when it rained and had minimal lighting for early-morning arrivals and late-evening departures. The college took action to pave and landscape the lot in 2002, adding directional signage for students and sufficient lighting. Once SFCC demonstrated it was listening to and acting on students' concerns in this area, their satisfaction with safety and security improved—from 4.54 in 2000 to 4.75 in 2003.

Satisfaction and Student Performance

As the preceding examples show, by listening to students' voices and addressing their concerns through an intentional and coordinated collegewide effort, SFCC was able to improve student satisfaction. Now, the critical question: How did improved student satisfaction affect student outcomes such as retention and graduation rates? Over the four years represented by SSI data, SFCC improved fall-to-fall student retention among associate of arts students from 60 to 75 percent. SFCC's most academically disadvantaged students—those in precollege or developmental classes—increased their success rate on the Florida-mandated course exit exam from 53 to 65 percent. The proportion of associate of arts students who completed their degree within four years increased from 25 to 32 percent. It would be impossible to claim a direct cause-and-effect relationship between the increase in student satisfaction at SFCC and the improvement in all of these traditional measurements of institutional effectiveness. However, it is undeniable that SFCC has experienced a concurrent improvement in both satisfaction and performance, and it is likely that these positive changes are interrelated. In simpler terms: student satisfaction matters.

Transforming College Culture

Community colleges were founded with a clear mission that remains to this day: to serve the diverse students who file through their open doors and prepare them for success in university transfer, career, or lifelong learning goals. Students come with the expectation that the community college will provide the path to these goals. The perceptions that students gather while on this path undeniably affect their engagement with the academic community as well as their likelihood to persist, succeed, and reach their goals. To meet and positively shape these perceptions, and to fulfill its mission, SFCC has realized that it must listen closely to students' voices so that these voices can inform the college's planning and decision making. By engaging in a true process of reflection and innovation, Santa Fe Community College has been able to renew its commitment to the principles of the learning college, increasing not just student satisfaction but also the likelihood that students will persist in achieving their academic aspirations.

NEW DIRECTIONS FOR COMMUNITY COLLEGES • DOI: 10.1002/cc

References

Astin, A. W. *What Matters in College: Four Critical Years Revisited.* San Francisco: Jossey-Bass, 1993.

Chickering, A., and Kytle, J. "The Collegiate Ideal in the Twenty-First Century." In J. D. Toma and A. J. Kezar (eds.), *Reconceptualizing the Collegiate Ideal.* New Directions for Higher Education, no. 105. San Francisco: Jossey-Bass, 1999.

Levine, A., and Cureton, J. *When Hope and Fear Collide: A Portrait of Today's College Student.* San Francisco: Jossey-Bass, 1998.

Noel-Levitz. *National Student Satisfaction Report, 2003.* Iowa City: Noel-Levitz, 2003. (ED 479 160)

Strange, C., and Banning, J. *Educating by Design: Creating Campus Learning Environments That Work.* San Francisco: Jossey-Bass, 2001.

ANNE M. KRESS *is interim vice president for academic affairs at Santa Fe Community College in Gainesville, Florida.*

NEW DIRECTIONS FOR COMMUNITY COLLEGES • DOI: 10.1002/cc

Using results from the Community College Survey of Student Engagement, community colleges can benchmark their performance with peer institutions on key indicators related to teaching, learning, and retention. This chapter offers an overview of the benchmarks and a focus on the challenges ahead.

Benchmarking Effective Educational Practice

Kay M. McClenney

Community colleges now enroll almost half of the students in U.S. undergraduate education, and they also serve disproportionately high numbers of low-income, first-generation, and minority students. Given the scope and the societal importance of the community college task, it is difficult to overstate the importance of assessing and strengthening the quality of educational practice in these institutions. Because community colleges have such a strong local focus, and because data about their performance have historically been scarce at best, there is a significant need for benchmarks of educational quality that are appropriate for these important institutions.

The Community College Survey of Student Engagement

The Community College Survey of Student Engagement (CCSSE) provides information about effective educational practice in community colleges and assists institutions in using that information to promote improvements in student learning and persistence. Established in 2001 as part of the Community College Leadership Program at the University of Texas at Austin, CCSSE's goal is to provide member colleges with results that can be used to inform decision making and target institutional improvement.

Providing the foundation for CCSSE's work is the concept of student engagement—that is, the amount of time and energy that students invest in

NEW DIRECTIONS FOR COMMUNITY COLLEGES, no. 134, Summer 2006   © Wiley Periodicals, Inc.
Published online in Wiley InterScience (www.interscience.wiley.com) • DOI: 10.1002/cc.236

47

educationally meaningful activities. CCSSE's survey instrument, the Community College Student Report, is designed to capture student engagement as a measure of institutional quality. Survey items are based on research about educational practices and student behaviors related to student persistence and student learning (Astin, 1993; Kuh, 2001a, 2001b; Pace, 1980; Pascarella and Terenzini, 2005; Tinto, 1993). For example, a large and growing body of research shows that active and collaborative learning, student-faculty interaction, high expectations, time on task, and regular, prompt feedback on academic performance are all important factors in promoting learning and student development.

Upon completion of its third national administration (in spring 2005), CCSSE had surveyed almost 400,000 students enrolled in 404 community and technical colleges in forty-three states, which represents 36 percent of the nation's community colleges and 37 percent of community college credit students. The participating community colleges are representative of the national group in terms of enrollment size (ranging from extra-large to small) and location (urban, suburban, or rural).

Because CCSSE uses random sampling procedures, student respondents generally reflect the underlying population of students in participating colleges (as well as the national community college student population) in terms of gender, race and ethnicity, and other characteristics. In the stratified random cluster sample scheme, each class section is a cluster. While a potential disadvantage of cluster sampling is increased standard errors, that concern is offset by the opportunity to collect larger amounts of data, and standard errors decrease as a function of increased sample sizes (Levy and Lemeshow, 1999). CCSSE's use of an in-class administration process substantially increases sample sizes and thus justifies the use of cluster sampling (Marti, 2005). Class sections to be surveyed are randomly selected from an electronic data file listing all credit courses offered at a participating college during the academic term in which the survey is conducted. Stratification is based on the time of day the class begins (morning, afternoon, or evening), ensuring that the number of courses in each time period in the sample is proportional to the total number offered during that time period. Because CCSSE samples classes rather than individual students, full-time students are overrepresented in the sample. For that reason, data are either disaggregated or weighted by part-time and full-time enrollment status so that the colleges' actual proportions of part- and full-time students are reflected in the results.

National Benchmarks of Effective Educational Practice

In 2003 CCSSE introduced to participating colleges and the public a set of five benchmarks of effective educational practice in community colleges.

NEW DIRECTIONS FOR COMMUNITY COLLEGES • DOI: 10.1002/cc

These important institutions, with missions focused on teaching, learning, and student success, may now gauge and monitor their performance in areas that are considered central to their work. In addition, participating colleges have the opportunity to make appropriate and useful comparisons between their performance and that of groups of similar colleges.

CCSSE's benchmarks are groups of conceptually related items that address key areas of student engagement, learning, and persistence that educational research has shown to be important in quality educational practice (Kuh, 2001a, 2001b; Pascarella and Terenzini, 2005). The five benchmarks of effective educational practice in community colleges are active and collaborative learning, student effort, academic challenge, student-faculty interaction, and support for learners. These benchmarks are tools that can be used to compare college performance in a number of useful ways, both within and across institutions. These five benchmarks will be described further in the following section.

The benchmarks were developed through factor analysis and expert judgment provided by CCSSE's technical advisory panel. Creation of benchmark scores involves rescaling items so that all are on the same scale and then standardizing the scores so that respondents' scores have a mean of fifty and a standard deviation of twenty-five. Rescaling the scores makes it possible to compare institutional performance across benchmarks and also facilitates benchmarking one college's performance against that of a selected group of institutions. Finally, benchmark scores are computed by averaging scores on the items comprising each benchmark.

In the standard benchmark reports provided to each participating college and also posted online (www.ccsse.org), CCSSE creates displays that enable each college to compare its own performance across benchmarks as well as to institutions of comparable size and to the full CCSSE population of community colleges. In addition, a decile report shows each college's relative performance on each of the benchmarks, with displays for all students and breakdowns by enrollment status (full- or part-time) and credit hours earned (up to twenty-nine credits, or thirty or more credits).

Within the "members only" section of the CCSSE Web site, community college leaders can use an interactive data-search capability to generate custom reports comparing their own college's performance at the benchmark and item levels to any other group of colleges—for example, to all other large urban (or small rural) colleges, to all of the participating colleges in the state or accrediting region, or to a self-selected peer group of three or more institutions. Armed with these benchmarking tools, community colleges have an opportunity to obtain systematic evidence about their students' educational experiences, examine differences among various students' experiences, benchmark effective educational practice, establish targets for excellence, and use their new understanding to focus and refine efforts to improve student success.

NEW DIRECTIONS FOR COMMUNITY COLLEGES • DOI: 10.1002/cc

CCSSE's National Benchmarks

The Community College Survey of Student Engagement's five benchmarks encompass thirty-eight engagement items that reflect many of the most important aspects of the student experience (Community College Survey of Student Engagement, 2003). These institutional practices and student behaviors are some of the more powerful contributors to effective educational practices in teaching, learning, and student retention (Astin, 1993; Kuh, 2001a, 2001b; Pace, 1980; Pascarella and Terenzini, 2005; Tinto, 1993). Each benchmark is briefly described here (see www.ccsse.org for more detailed information).

Active and Collaborative Learning. Students typically learn more when they are actively involved in their education and have opportunities to think about and apply what they are learning in different settings. Through collaboration with others to solve problems or master content, students develop valuable skills that prepare them to deal with the kinds of situations and problems they will encounter in the workplace, the community, and in their personal lives. The survey items that contribute to this benchmark ask, for example, how often students have participated in a variety of activities during the current college year. These activities include asking questions in class or participating in class discussions, working with other students on projects in class or outside of class, tutoring other students, and participating in a community-based project as part of their coursework.

Student Effort. Students' own behaviors contribute significantly to their learning and to the chances that they will persist in college and attain their educational goals. Quite obviously, time on task is critically important, and there are a number of ways that a student's investment of time and level of effort may be assessed. This benchmark comprises eight survey items that ask, for example, how often the student has prepared two or more drafts of an assignment before turning it in, how frequently they come to class unprepared, how often they used tutor services or the computer lab, and so forth. Other items ask how many unassigned books the student read during the current school year and how many hours the student spends preparing for class in a typical week.

Academic Challenge. The level of rigor incorporated into students' academic work is a key element of collegiate quality and individual learning. Ten items from the CCSSE survey address aspects of academic challenge, including the nature and amount of assigned academic work (reading and writing), the complexity of cognitive tasks presented to students, and the level of challenge experienced through faculty evaluations of student performance.

Student-Faculty Interaction. The more contact students have with their teachers, the more likely they are to learn effectively and persist toward achievement of their educational goals. Personal interaction with faculty members strengthens students' connections to the college and helps them focus on their academic progress. Working with an instructor on a project or serving with faculty members on a college committee lets students see first-hand how experts identify and solve practical problems. Through such interactions, faculty members become role models, mentors, and guides for continuous, lifelong learning. The six items used in this benchmark include queries about students' experience using e-mail to communicate with an instructor, discussing grades or assignments with an instructor, discussing ideas from readings or classes with instructors outside of class, and receiving prompt feedback on academic performance.

Support for Learners. Students perform better and are more satisfied at colleges that are committed to their success and that cultivate positive working and social relationships among different groups on campus. Community college students also benefit from services that assist them with academic and career planning, academic skill development, and other issues that may affect both learning and retention. The seven survey items contributing to this benchmark ask students about the frequency with which they use certain services and about the extent to which the college provides the support needed to help students succeed. The survey also asks how well the college encourages contact among students from different economic, social, and racial or ethnic backgrounds and how well it provides financial support for meeting college costs.

Using the Benchmarks

There are a number of ways that college leaders, faculty, and staff can use the benchmarks and comparison information provided both on the CCSSE Web site and in the standard benchmark reports.

Explore Survey Results. Where does one start in the effort to grapple with large amounts of data gathered from a significant number of students? The benchmark scores point to a handful of important areas that begin to tell the story of student experiences in a given institution. Typically, a college will perform well on some benchmarks and not so well on others, leading users to question what might explain the differences. Or the college may have an effort under way—perhaps an initiative to strengthen critical thinking across the curriculum—and will use the scores to see whether the work appears to be reflected in results on the academic challenge benchmark.

Paint the Big Picture. Understanding student engagement may begin with a review of how the college is performing overall, followed by an examination of results broken down by enrollment status (full- versus part-time students) and credit hours earned (fewer than thirty credit hours versus thirty or more credit hours). At this point, college administrators, faculty, and staff will begin to see that the student experience is not monolithic; indeed, it varies significantly across subgroups of students.

Identify Key Findings. Benchmark scores (and results on items comprising the benchmarks) can be used to focus college attention on educational practices, programs, and policies that may be in need of improvement—and on those worthy of celebration. Faculty and staff may discover things that surprise them (for example, that students do not write as much as faculty think they should), or they may confirm through CCSSE findings a focus that they already knew (or at least suspected) should be a priority (for example, establishing learning communities in order to promote active and collaborative learning).

Make Institutional Comparisons. The American Productivity and Quality Center (APQC) was an early pioneer in the process of benchmarking for quality improvement. According to APQC (2000), benchmarking requires "being humble enough to admit that someone else is better at something and wise enough to learn how to match, or even surpass them at it" (p. 1). As noted above, CCSSE employs a strict sampling protocol that allows for appropriate institutional comparisons. After identifying other colleges that are high performers on a particular benchmark, a college team can initiate communication to explore the educational practices that may be contributing to enhanced effectiveness at benchmark institutions. Visiting benchmark institutions can be highly productive and helpful in improving practice in one's own college. Augmenting the benchmarking options is the opportunity for colleges to join CCSSE as part of a consortium (five or more colleges with common interests, challenges, or characteristics). Each consortium may add up to fifteen customized questions to the survey, and CCSSE provides consortium benchmarks in a supplementary report.

Further Inquiry. CCSSE's benchmark scores can also be used in conjunction with other institutional data in order to investigate factors contributing to student success. For example, examining the relationship between student engagement and successful course completion, grade point average, persistence, and graduation—and disaggregating results to understand the disparate experiences of certain student groups—may prompt important campus discussions and ultimately support significant improvements in programs and services for students.

Accountability and Accreditation

From the outset, CCSSE has been committed to public reporting of survey results, and each participating college president signs an agreement about both public reporting and responsible uses of survey results. This agreement reflects a significant commitment to both transparency and improvement, and there is no evidence that the reporting requirement has had a significant negative effect on participation in the survey. Furthermore, reactions from public leaders and the media have been overwhelmingly positive. CCSSE's benchmarking capabilities have made it a valuable tool in regional accreditation and state accountability processes that increasingly call for a focus on student learning and success and very often require some use of assessments that involve comparison to national norms or benchmarks. The emphasis on assessment as a tool for quality improvement is completely aligned with CCSSE's purposes.

NEW DIRECTIONS FOR COMMUNITY COLLEGES • DOI: 10.1002/cc

Public reporting is accomplished via the CCSSE Web site at www.ccsse.org. The site provides general information about community colleges and student engagement, a description of the survey sampling and administration processes, and tools for understanding and using survey results. In addition, each participating college has a profile page that not only displays survey results and institutional information, but also provides an important context for interpreting the data.

Caveats and Cautionary Notes

When used appropriately, benchmarking can be an effective tool for institutional improvement. For community colleges, the central focus is on improvement of student learning, persistence, and attainment. Still, two-year colleges differ significantly from one another, and there is dramatic variation in terms of size, geographic location, available resources, institutional priorities, enrollment patterns, programs, and student characteristics. These differences must be taken into account in the benchmarking process, both when interpreting an individual institution's benchmark scores and especially when making institutional comparisons. The CCSSE Web site assists users in making appropriate comparisons by providing key information about the participating colleges and their student populations and by allowing users to benchmark their college's performance against the aggregate results for a comparison group (comprised of at least three other colleges) chosen by the user.

CCSSE is flatly opposed to college rankings, which are statistically inappropriate. The CCSSE National Advisory Board and CCSSE's cosponsor, the Carnegie Foundation for the Advancement of Teaching, have clearly stated their conviction that reducing student engagement to a single indicator obscures complex dimensions of institutional performance and student behavior. For this reason, rankings are inherently flawed as a tool for accountability and improvement, no matter the information on which they are based. In sum, CCSSE affirms the importance of public accountability for quality in higher education and strongly supports efforts to improve educational practice; ranking colleges serves neither purpose.

Reaching for Excellence

Benchmarking college performance against a national average, or against the average for groups of similar institutions, is a useful starting point. But it does not push colleges to reach for excellence—that is, to look past average scores when it comes to promoting student learning and persistence. Unfortunately, many national averages—whether for student-faculty interaction or for graduation rates—are generally not at the level where they need to be (McClenney, 2004). Thus, community college educators must continually ask a series of courageous questions: Is our current performance good enough? Is the national average is good enough? How good, for that matter, is *good enough?*

To support these conversations on individual campuses, CCSSE (2004) has proposed five ways in which community colleges might reach for excellence in student engagement. To begin, colleges can compare their performance to the national average. Second, community colleges may compare themselves to high-performing institutions. A college might, for example, aspire to improve its performance to a point at or above the eighty-fifth percentile on some or all of the benchmarks. Third, colleges may measure their overall performance against results for their least-engaged group. That is, a community college might seek to ensure that all student groups (for example, full- and part-time students, students in developmental sequences, and students from all racial, ethnic, and income groups) are engaged in their education at similarly high levels. Fourth, two-year colleges may focus their benchmarking efforts in areas of high priority in the institution's strategic plan or on issues the college community strongly values. For example, an institution might zero in on survey items related to services for first-generation college students or on the academic challenge benchmark. Finally, colleges may—and should—make the most important comparison of all: How are they performing now, compared to how they want to be? By benchmarking against its own baseline performance, a college can pursue a commitment to continuous improvement over time.

As CCSSE colleges become more experienced in benchmarking performance and using data to target institutional improvement, it becomes apparent that there are a few key themes that characterize effective efforts. First, it is important that faculty and other key groups on campus are involved early and often in the decision to use the engagement survey and in subsequent reviews and interpretation of results. Involving all college constituents in the process of discovering issues for themselves (rather than being told what the issues are) is an effective way to initiate change. Second, data are most useful when they provide answers to questions people care about. Thus, it helps to focus on results and benchmarking projects that illuminate issues of concern to the campus community—even when the data may contradict common wisdom. For example, although faculty members may recognize the importance of student-faculty interaction, and though an individual teacher's experience may suggest that she is frequently interacting with students, the systematically collected data will often show that the typical student experience is far less engaging than faculty members estimate. Third, benchmarking aligns with the reality that most people want to be involved with high-quality organizations that do high-quality work. Therefore, when faculty and student service professionals in community colleges see evidence that shows them the way to improve outcomes for students, they are often eager to move from discussion to action.

An inescapable conclusion drawn from CCSSE's findings and its work with participating colleges is that engagement is important to the success of community college students, but it is also challenging to ensure. Because community college students juggle multiple responsibilities—families, jobs, and community obligations—in addition to their studies, because they commute to college and tend to leave campus after class, and because they bring multiple challenges to college with them, engagement does not happen by accident (Community College Survey of Student Engagement, 2004). Rather, it has to happen by design. Given this reality, community colleges are called upon to rethink and redesign educational experiences for students, making connection and engagement virtually inescapable. Benchmarking can be a valuable tool in helping community colleges rise to that challenge.

References

American Productivity and Quality Center. *APQC Benchmarking Methodology*. Houston, Tex.: American Productivity and Quality Center, 2000. http://www.apqc.org/portal/apqc/site/generic?path=/site/benchmarking/methodologies.jhtml. Accessed Feb. 12, 2006.

Astin, A. W. *What Matters in College? Four Critical Years Revisited*. San Francisco: Jossey-Bass, 1993.

Community College Survey of Student Engagement. *Engaging Community Colleges: National Benchmarks of Quality, 2003 Findings*. Austin, Tex.: Community College Survey of Student Engagement, 2003. http://www.ccsse.org/publications/report2003.pdf. Accessed Feb. 12, 2006.

Community College Survey of Student Engagement. *Engagement by Design, 2004 Findings*. Austin, Tex.: Community College Survey of Student Engagement, 2004. http://www.ccsse.org/publications/CCSSE_reportfinal2004.pdf. Accessed Feb. 12, 2006.

Kuh, G. D. "Assessing What Really Matters to Student Learning." *Change*, 2001a, *33*(3), 10–17, 66.

Kuh, G. D. "The National Survey of Student Engagement: Conceptual Framework and Overview of Psychometric Properties." Bloomington: Indiana University, Center for Postsecondary Research and Planning, 2001b. http://nsse.iub.edu/nsse_2001/pdf/framework-2001.pdf. Accessed Feb. 12, 2006.

Levy, P. S., and Lemeshow, S. *Sampling of Populations: Methods and Applications*. New York: Wiley, 1999.

Marti, C. N. "Dimensions of Student Engagement in American Community Colleges: Using the Community College Student Report in Research and Practice." Unpublished manuscript, 2005. http://www.ccsse.org/aboutsurvey/psychometrics.pdf. Accessed Feb. 14, 2006.

McClenney, K. M. "Keeping America's Promise: Challenges for Community Colleges." In K. Boswell and C. D. Wilson (eds.), *Keeping America's Promise: A Report on the Future of the Community College*. Denver, Colo.: Education Commission of the States, 2004. http://www.league.org/league/projects/promise/files/promise.pdf. Accessed Feb. 12, 2006.

Pace, C. R. *Measuring the Quality of Student Effort*. Current Issues in Higher Education, no. 2. Washington, D.C.: American Association for Higher Education, 1980.

Pascarella, E., and Terenzini, P. *How College Affects Students: A Third Decade of Research*. San Francisco: Jossey-Bass, 2005.

Tinto, V. *Leaving College: Rethinking the Causes and Cures of Student Attrition*. Chicago: University of Chicago Press, 1993.

KAY M. MCCLENNEY *is director of the Community College Survey of Student Engagement, part of the Community College Leadership Program at the University of Texas at Austin.*

NEW DIRECTIONS FOR COMMUNITY COLLEGES • DOI: 10.1002/cc

This chapter describes how Tallahassee Community College used CCSSE data as part of its overall student-retention program, consisting of faculty workshops, analysis of state accountability data, and conscious incorporation of best practices. The resulting Quality Enhancement Plan (QEP) meets accreditation requirements and strengthens the college's strategic plan.

Using CCSSE in Planning for Quality Enhancement

Scott E. Balog, Sally P. Search

Tallahassee Community College (TCC) is a comprehensive community college with a strong transfer program (80 percent of its students are enrolled in an associate of arts degree program), a variety of vocational programs, and a growing workforce-development program. The college was recently listed twenty-second among the nation's top producers of associate of arts degrees, and a majority of TCC's graduates transfer to neighboring Florida State University. TCC also maintains an excellent relationship with Florida A&M as well as other universities throughout the state; nearly three-fourths of the college's associate degree recipients transfer into the state university system. In addition, TCC enrolls one of the highest percentages of African American students in Florida and confers a greater percentage of associate degrees on African American students than any other two-year institution in the state.

Despite these successes, state accountability data revealed areas of concern related to how well TCC students were prepared when they transferred to the state university system. Data showed that the number of TCC students maintaining a 2.5 grade point average in upper-division courses lagged considerably behind the state average. In addition, that percentage declined sharply between 2001 and 2002, reaching its lowest point since 1996. Disparities between minority and white students were also evident in these data. Moreover, among Florida students who took the College Level Academic Skills Test (a test required for graduation with an associate degree in Florida) in 2002–03, TCC ranked twenty-sixth out of twenty-eight community

NEW DIRECTIONS FOR COMMUNITY COLLEGES, no. 134, Summer 2006   © Wiley Periodicals, Inc.
Published online in Wiley InterScience (www.interscience.wiley.com) • DOI: 10.1002/cc.236

colleges on the essay, twenty-fifth on English language skills, twenty-fourth in reading, and thirteenth in mathematics. Rather than hiding or ignoring these areas of concern, TCC administrators, faculty, and staff acknowledged the deficiencies and actively discussed and researched methods to improve student success as part of a larger process to enhance the quality of the college's instruction and student support.

As part of the reaffirmation of accreditation process, colleges and universities accredited by the Southern Association of Colleges and Schools, including TCC, are required to develop a Quality Enhancement Plan (QEP) that is designed to improve student learning outcomes. The QEP must employ a focused course of action that is empirically based and engages the entire campus community. The QEP's focus should be determined by an analysis of the educational landscape to assess strengths, weaknesses, and opportunities for enhancing college practices that contribute to student retention and success, and the QEP should address issues of importance to the institution. The development of the QEP became an integral part of TCC's planning and assessment process, as it would not only satisfy the requirements for reaffirmation of accreditation, but would also help build a campus culture committed to student learning, development, retention, and success. In order to assess and analyze its learning environment and to aid the institution in formulating its QEP, TCC began administering the Community College Survey of Student Engagement (CCSSE), results of which served as a catalyst to more effectively engage students and enhance performance outcomes. The following section describes the data used to formulate TCC's Quality Enhancement Plan. The next sections describe the QEP framework and the ways in which CCSSE data and the QEP plan have been used to improve student retention. The chapter concludes with a discussion of how these elements have all become a part of TCC's strategic plan.

Assessing and Analyzing the Campus Learning Environment: Elements Informing TCC's Quality Enhancement Plan

In order to develop its quality enhancement plan, TCC first carefully analyzed the campus learning environment by examining the college's student success initiative (called EagleEYE), results from the CCSSE, other empirical data related to student engagement and success, feedback from faculty workshops on student success, and finally, scholarly research and best practices in student success and engagement. Analyzing institutional data that did not mirror the image of TCC held by many faculty and administrators was often a difficult and uncomfortable task. TCC is, by many measures, a high-performing institution, yet CCSSE and other data revealed gaps that were impossible to ignore.

EagleEYE. In spring 2000, TCC began a campuswide student retention study that would later emerge as a comprehensive student success initiative known as EagleEYE (Enhance Your Education). The primary purpose of EagleEYE was to develop a system of coordinated, institutionalized programs that resulted in student success and learning. Central to this initiative is what the college calls the Teacher-Learner Continuum, which describes the changing relationship between teachers and learners as students develop and mature and is discussed in more detail in the next section. Since EagleEYE's inception, TCC has worked diligently to streamline programs and services, blurring boundaries that once produced factions among academic and student services and created barriers to student progression and success. The college's collaborative focus on its student success initiative has helped advance students in their development as proficient learners.

CCSSE Findings. Results from TCC's first administration of CCSSE in spring 2003 played an important role in informing decisions about the QEP. Based on 965 student responses to the survey, TCC faculty and administrators learned that the college had many areas of strength in serving and engaging students. However, the college also identified six areas in need of improvement. Based on a four-point Likert-type scale (where 1 = never, 2 = sometimes, 3 = often, and 4 = very often), students' responses to the CCSSE suggested institutional challenges in students' class participation (the institutional average was 2.67) and class preparation (2.26), peer collaboration (2.30), assessment and prompt feedback (2.58), and emphasis on higher-order thinking skills (2.55). In addition, on a separate Likert-type scale (that ranged from 1 = the institution is unfriendly and unsupportive; I have a sense of alienation to 7 = the institution is friendly and supportive; I have a sense of belonging), students' average responses to questions about the quality of relationships among students (5.18) and between faculty and students (5.39) signaled a need for improvement. On these measures, TCC scored substantially below the average of other large colleges ($p < .001$).

The CCSSE data were of particular value and importance to faculty and staff because they represented students' experiences in classes and on campus. Furthermore, they identified issues that faculty and staff felt empowered to address in meaningful ways. Unlike accountability data that track the retention and success of cohorts of students whose experiences at the college took place before many of the strategies articulated in EagleEYE were implemented, the insights gleaned from CCSSE speak to present-day perceptions of students' experiences. In addition, the CCSSE report allowed TCC to compare its results related to the success of applied engagement strategies with those of other community colleges at both regional and national levels that were similar in size and with similar demographics.

Other Empirical Data. In addition to CCSSE data, TCC analyzed empirical data related to state accountability measures, such as course completion, student retention and withdrawal, and graduation rates. While TCC's analysis produced many positive findings, the college also discovered several areas of concern. In 2002, TCC students' rate of successful completion of developmental coursework lagged behind the state average, as did graduation rates for both associate of arts and associate of science degrees. Of particular concern to TCC faculty and staff was the disparity between the success of white and African American students. Additional data compiled by the Southern Regional Education Board for the 2002–03 school year indicated that for the two-year persistence rate, TCC ranked twenty-sixth out of twenty-eight community colleges in Florida. For the three-year completion and retention rate, TCC ranked twentieth, and for the completion within 150 percent of the expected time-to-completion measure, TCC ranked twenty-fifth. Despite TCC's efforts to increase student success, these data demonstrated that students were not persisting or completing their educational objectives to the degree TCC expected.

Faculty and Staff Workshops. One of the challenges in developing a QEP or any collegewide initiative is ensuring that all members of the college community have an opportunity to provide input and are able to contribute to the resulting plan. At the beginning of the fall 2003 semester, TCC held a QEP retreat for faculty, learning center specialists, and student affairs staff to dissect CCSSE and state accountability data and to identify student success themes. Approximately 175 faculty and staff divided into small groups to examine how the data could be addressed and were asked to respond to several questions adapted from the League for Innovation in the Community College's Vanguard Learning College Project. Specifically, groups were asked to address the following questions: What student behaviors are most critically related to student retention and positive learning outcomes? How can TCC effectively assess, benchmark, monitor, and improve student engagement in learning, and what performance indicators will help TCC know how effective its approaches really are? What structures, policies, and processes have proven to be most critical in promoting the success of underprepared students at TCC? Finally, what are the keys to creating information systems to track student progress and success at TCC?

Discussions in faculty and staff work groups began to coalesce around the concept of improving student success through increased student engagement in the learning process, with an emphasis on shared responsibilities between students and the college, clearly defined student goals and outcomes, early intervention strategies, progressive academic advising, campus collaboration, and prompt communication and feedback. CCSSE results provided clear direction in targeting programs and services to meet student needs and allowed for future assessments via subsequent administrations of the survey.

Scholarly Research and Best Practices. In addition to analyzing CCSSE and other data and taking into account feedback from faculty and staff, the QEP steering committee spent much of the fall 2003 semester reading and discussing relevant research and articles related to best practices in quality enhancement and student engagement. Subcommittees identified best practices, relevant conferences and workshops, research, and informative readings. All members of the committee read assigned articles, and facilitators summarized and led discussions. Readings such as "Student Success

NEW DIRECTIONS FOR COMMUNITY COLLEGES • DOI: 10.1002/cc

and the Building of Involving Education Communities" (Tinto, 2002), "Toward Learning from Engagement" (Elsner, 2002), "Toward a New Way of Thinking and Learning: Becoming a Learning College" (Atkins and Wolfe, 2003), and "Learning Communities at the Community College" (Minkler, 2002) guided the committee in its initial discussions about how to increase the college's emphasis on student engagement and individualized learning.

Continued discussions concentrated on a range of topics associated with the committee's broad definition of learning outcomes. The committee examined both theoretical and practical outcomes that could be attained through institutional commitment to strategies for increasing student retention, improving the success of first-generation and minority students, incorporating active learning techniques, developing a sense of community, and improving students' ability to think critically and reflectively. As discussions evolved, the focus became clear: student engagement would be the primary vehicle for improving students' learning outcomes along the Teacher-Learner continuum. In addition, the committee concluded that successful education is a shared responsibility between both the teacher and learner. This was an important realization, as part of the institutional challenge in developing the QEP was to develop strategies that empower students to be the architects of their own success.

The QEP Conceptual Framework

After TCC faculty and staff determined that the focus of the QEP would be increasing student success through student engagement and responsibility, the committee began to articulate a conceptual framework to guide the development and implementation of strategies and to provide a context for discussion with the campus as a whole. This framework consisted of the following components.

Teacher-Learner Continuum. To a large extent, the QEP is an outgrowth of EagleEYE, and the Teacher-Learner continuum is central to the philosophy underlying both initiatives. The Teacher-Learner continuum describes the relationship between the learner and the teacher as the learner progresses through a series of developmental stages from novice to independent, self-actualized learner.

Embodied in the Teacher-Learner continuum is a commitment to address student needs and, through engagement and shared responsibility, to improve the educational experience for all students. Students' development along the Teacher-Learner continuum can, to a large extent, be understood by examining their responses to items on the CCSSE. Responses to survey items related to students' opinions about the school, students' educational and personal growth, and the college's student services are beneficial not only because they offer administrators and faculty quantifiable measures of utilization of campus programs, services, and resources, but also because they provide insight into students' awareness and willingness to use such offerings. Moreover, an analysis of students' responses to survey items related to college activities and to questions about issues that could cause them to withdraw allowed TCC to identify areas where TCC must make a concerted effort to improve students' experiences, development, and retention.

To guide the development of student engagement initiatives, TCC integrated two other sets of principles into the QEP framework. In particular, the college adapted principles from O'Banion's book, *A Learning College for the 21st Century* (1997) and Chickering and Gamson's article, "Seven Principles for Good Practice in Undergraduate Education" (1987).

Learning College Principles. The principles of the learning college (O'Banion, 1997) emphasize student responsibility and learning as a collaborative process. These principles were important in light of CCSSE data that indicated both a lack of student responsibility in some areas and a lack of collaborative learning experiences at TCC.

Seven Principles for Good Practice in Undergraduate Education. Chickering and Gamson's (1987) seven principles for good practice in undergraduate education underlie effective classroom education and address many of the challenges identified in TCC's CCSSE results.

Using CCSSE and the QEP to Improve Retention

The QEP steering committee recognized that to have a significant effect on student learning outcomes, the college must take steps to integrate students into the institution, both socially and academically. Retention is critical, but the committee concurred with Tinto (2002), who observed that successful education is the secret of successful retention programs. Institutional success, he states, "resides in the work of the faculty and the institution's capacity to construct educational communities that actively engage students in learning. It lies not in the retention of students but in their education" (p. 1). Thus, two of the QEP's core initiatives focus on teaching and learning. However, the QEP also includes five initiatives in the areas of early intervention, communication, and collaboration that are essential to providing successful education. In order to actively engage students in the learning process, TCC must have a campus culture and infrastructure that can foster social and intellectual growth.

To increase students' academic and social integration and to improve learning outcomes, TCC's quality-enhancement plan focuses on increasing student engagement through seven initiatives that fall into three interrelated categories, as illustrated in Figure 6.1. Collectively, these initiatives respond to and address the issues raised by accountability data, CCSSE data, Eagle-EYE, and feedback from faculty and staff.

Two initiatives that have a direct effect on student learning outcomes are teaching and learning; in these instances CCSSE data provided valuable insight into students' experiences and had a significant impact on both the

Figure 6.1. Tallahassee Community College's QEP Model

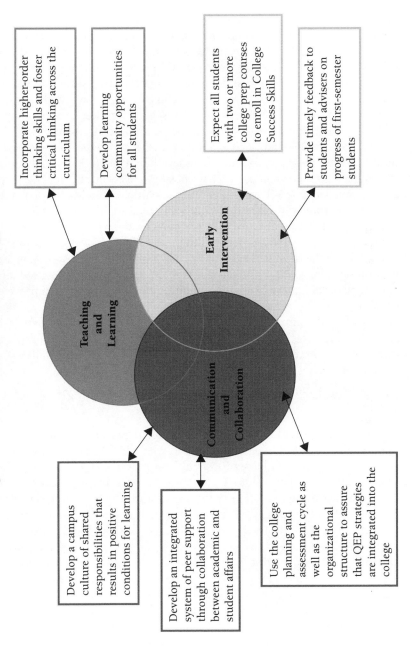

Incorporate higher-order thinking skills and foster critical thinking across the curriculum

Develop learning community opportunities for all students

Expect all students with two or more college prep courses to enroll in College Success Skills

Provide timely feedback to students and advisers on progress of first-semester students

Early Intervention

Teaching and Learning

Communication and Collaboration

Develop a campus culture of shared responsibilities that results in positive conditions for learning

Develop an integrated system of peer support through collaboration between academic and student affairs

Use the college planning and assessment cycle as well as the organizational structure to assure that QEP strategies are integrated into the college direction and substance of the college's QEP. CCSSE data also indicated a need to help students develop and use higher-order thinking skills. A well-defined, adaptable program that builds on TCC's areas of strength, emphasizes reading and writing, and requires students to think critically and creatively to synthesize, integrate, and apply information to new and different situations could provide many opportunities to address the challenges so clearly outlined in the CCSSE data. To meet its teaching and learning objectives, the college revised program goals to include higher-order thinking skills and modified the master syllabi to include learning outcomes, assignments, and assessment measures that reflect those skills. TCC's goal for the immediate future includes revising all individual course syllabi in much the same way.

CCSSE data also indicated a need to provide students with greater opportunities for meaningful collaboration. Research by Tinto (2002) clearly demonstrates that learning communities have positive effects on student engagement and success. He observed that students who participate in learning communities are better integrated into the college, both academically and socially. In addition, students are afforded greater opportunities for making connections between ideas and concepts, for thinking critically, and for collaborating with others. Given the proven benefits associated with student immersion in learning communities, TCC created a carefully designed program focused on the continued development of learning communities. In an effort to improve peer collaboration, class participation, and the quality of relationships among students and faculty (areas for improvement that were identified in an analysis of students' responses to the CCSSE survey), TCC hopes to incorporate interdivisional collaboration into half of its learning communities by fall 2007.

Integrating CCSSE and the QEP into TCC's Strategic Plan

TCC's development of its QEP depended largely on results from the college's first administration of CCSSE in spring 2003. In combination with state accountability data and a synthesis of best practices related to providing quality academic programs, TCC's QEP focuses on increasing student engagement through seven initiatives that fall into three interrelated categories. Each of the seven QEP initiatives is tied to one of the priority initiatives in the college's strategic plan. This plan consists of the college's mission statement, four primary goals relating to teaching, campus, community, and students, and twenty priority initiatives and associated strategic initiatives. The priority initiatives address five college principles: innovation, diversity, excellence, access, and success. Expected learning outcomes, primary student success and engagement indicators, and associated budget allocations are also identified in the plan. CCSSE data serve as primary student success and engagement indicators in five of the seven QEP initiatives. Integrating the QEP into the strategic plan ensures that the implementation and effectiveness of the initiatives are assessed on a regular and predictable basis.

TCC prides itself on offering its students high-quality postsecondary educational opportunities and providing optimal conditions for student learning. Assessment tools like CCSSE provide the college with an effective way to measure the programs and services that are established to engage students and promote retention and success. To ensure that the college continues to adequately meet students' needs and to help in its transition to a learning college, TCC will continue to administer the CCSSE for years to come.

References

Atkins, S., and Wolfe, C. "Toward a New Way of Thinking and Learning: Becoming a Learning College." *Learning Abstracts,* 2003, 6(10). http://www.league.org/publication/abstracts/learning/lelabs0309.htm. Accessed Feb. 27, 2006.

Chickering, A. W., and Gamson, Z. F. "Seven Principles for Good Practice in Undergraduate Education." *AAHE Bulletin,* 1987, 39(7), 3–7.

Elsner, P. A. "Toward Learning from Engagement." *Community College Journal,* 2002, 72(5), 16–21.

Minkler, J. E. "Learning Communities at the Community College." *Community College Review,* 2002, 30(3), 46–63.

O'Banion, T. *A Learning College for the 21st Century.* Phoenix, Ariz.: American Council on Education/Oryx Press, 1997.

Tinto, V. "Student Success and the Building of Involving Educational Communities." Syracuse, N.Y.: Syracuse University, 2002. http://soeweb.syr.edu/Faculty/Vtinto/Files/PromotingStudentSuccess.pdf. Accessed Feb. 27, 2006.

SCOTT E. BALOG is assistant to the president at Tallahassee Community College (Florida).

SALLY P. SEARCH is professor of mathematics and former director of the Center for Teaching Excellence at Tallahassee Community College (Florida).

7

The National Community College Benchmark Project (NCCBP) provides community colleges with a system to report data on key learning outcomes and indicators of institutional effectiveness and to compare their data with national norms and data from selected peer institutions. This chapter describes the development, current features, and anticipated enhancements of the NCCBP.

The National Community College Benchmark Project

Ralph Juhnke

As a result of growing enrollments, limited funding, and increased pressures for accountability from accrediting agencies, governing bodies, and other stakeholders, community colleges must demonstrate student attainment and institutional effectiveness by analyzing intra-institutional trends and inter-institutional comparisons. The National Community College Benchmark Project (NCCBP) was created to provide a national data collection and reporting process that enables community colleges to compare student outcomes and performance indicators with those of peer institutions. The project allows for systematic assessments of uniform performance measures within an institution and provides a means for comparing those measures with other colleges to identify performance similarities and differences.

NCCBP Development and the Community College Benchmark Task Force

In winter and spring 2003, representatives from eleven community colleges and a representative from the League for Innovation in the Community College met at Johnson County Community College (Kansas) to propose an approach to benchmarking community college outcomes, to identify and define benchmarks (both summary outcome and performance measures) and data elements (quantitative indicators of benchmark components), and to develop data collection and benchmark reporting processes. These representatives—collectively called the Community College Benchmark Task

Force—created benchmarks in commonly reported performance and outcome areas as well as areas of greatest strategic importance to their institutions. Benchmarks were proposed for areas of student performance, aspects of student satisfaction and engagement, career preparation, access and participation, and business-and-industry and organizational performance.

Student performance benchmarks include the following: completion rates (the proportions of full- and part-time students who complete degrees or certificates or who transfer to a senior institution), transfer-student performance (cumulative grade point average, average first-year credit hours, and second-year persistence rate at transfer institutions), and persistence rates (the proportion of credit students who persisted from one term to the next or from one fall to the next). Benchmarks related to student learning outcomes include the proportions of students who achieve their educational objective; retention and success rates for credit college-level courses; retention and success rates for credit developmental or remedial courses; retention and success rates of former credit developmental or remedial students in their first college-level courses; retention and success rates in four core academic skill areas; institution-wide grade distributions that indicate withdrawal, completion, and success rates and percentages of A and B grades; and institution-wide credit distance-learning grade distributions that indicate withdrawal, completion, and success rates and percentages of A and B grades.

Student satisfaction and engagement indicators include summary items from the Noel-Levitz Student Satisfaction Inventory, the ACT Student Opinion Survey, and summary benchmarks from the Community College Survey of Student Engagement. Career preparation benchmarks include the proportion of career-program completers who are either employed in a field related to their career program or pursuing additional education, as well as the proportion of employers who are satisfied with career-program completers' overall preparation. Access and participation benchmarks include the proportion of minority students and employees, the proportion of high school graduates from the college's services area who enroll at the institution, credit and non-credit students as a proportion of the service area population, and participants in institution-sponsored cultural activities, public meetings, and sporting events as a proportion of the service area population.

Finally, organizational performance indicators include the number of students enrolled in business and contract training classes, companies served, business-and-industry costs and revenues, average credit section size, student-to-faculty ratio, the proportion of credit hours and sections taught by full-time faculty, the proportion of total credit hours and sections that are administered at a distance, student-to-student services staff ratios, retirement and departure rates, grievance and harassment action rates, costs per credit hour and full-time-equivalent (FTE) student, and development or training expenditures per FTE employee.

NEW DIRECTIONS FOR COMMUNITY COLLEGES • DOI: 10.1002/cc

Participating in the NCCBP

Participation in the NCCBP begins when institutions send in a subscription form and pay an annual fee. On the subscription form, subscribers indicate their institutional type (single- or multicampus), campus environment (urban, suburban, or rural), institutional control (public, private, or proprietary), calendar (semester or quarter), and whether or not their faculty and staff are unionized. They also provide contact information and indicate agreement with data confidentiality and use policies. For example, all NCCBP data are confidential; no institutional identifying information is communicated except to individual subscribing institutions themselves. As well, both subscribers and NCCBP agree to make reasonable efforts to ensure that data are accurate. Reported data are to be used by subscribing institutions and should not be shared with unauthorized individuals.

Data Collection and Confirmation

NCCBP data collection begins annually in late winter and ends in September. The principal data collection instrument is a Microsoft Excel workbook that includes definitions of data elements, instructions, and data-entry forms on separate worksheets. The 2005 workbook contained twenty worksheets and twenty-seven forms. An example of the 2005 workbook is available on the NCCBP Web site (www.nccbp.org). Each worksheet includes formulas to calculate and display benchmark values based on data-element values, as well as validation messages to help ensure accurate entries. Data-element values in individual worksheets are recorded simultaneously on an additional summary worksheet at the back of the workbook. Completed workbooks are submitted as attachments to e-mail messages addressed to NCCBP staff.

As workbooks are received, data-element values on the summary worksheet are appended by a software application to the NCCBP database after it checks for inappropriate data types and missing and inconsistent data (values that do not conform to data-entry instructions). The application then creates Excel worksheets that list missing and inconsistent items and attaches those worksheets to e-mail messages that ask reporting institutions to provide or correct values. Because the process is automated, entry of data into the NCCBP database from an institution's workbook and delivery of a request to supply missing and check inconsistent values take less than one minute.

A second round of data confirmation occurs when all responding institutions have supplied missing data elements and corrected inconsistencies. In the second round, institutions' benchmark values are compared with means of values reported by all participants, and worksheets that report seriously divergent values are e-mailed with requests for verification. Updated benchmark values then become the bases for annual reports.

NEW DIRECTIONS FOR COMMUNITY COLLEGES • DOI: 10.1002/cc

NCCBP has completed two full-scale implementations of this evolving, national data collection and reporting system. In 2004, 110 community colleges participated in the project; 112 institutions participated in 2005. All of the 2005 participants were public, two-year institutions or multicollege districts, and most were on semester calendars. Their enrollments ranged from 900 to 120,000 (median = 6,500); larger institutions were multicollege districts. Participants were distributed fairly evenly across urban, suburban, and rural environments, and most (60 percent) were single-campus institutions. Participants are self-selected, and peer comparisons are designed for individual institutions' use. Therefore, NCCBP participants do not necessarily represent the national population of community colleges, and no claim of national representativeness is intended. Participants are distributed across the United States and include all thirty SUNY community colleges in New York, fourteen colleges in Arizona, all thirteen Tennessee community colleges, thirteen colleges in Pennsylvania, and eleven community colleges in Texas. In addition, all twenty-eight community colleges in the Florida State System will participate in the project in 2006.

Annual and Context Reports

Annual reports of aggregate data are prepared when participants have verified and updated data-element values. Aggregate reports include participating colleges' benchmark values and values at the 10th, 25th, 50th (median), 75th, and 90th percentiles of aggregate data. These reports are e-mailed to participating institutions at the end of the data collection period (in early fall). Participants are asked to verify again that reported benchmark values are correct or to report corrections. An example of the most recent annual aggregate report is available on the NCCBP Web site.

NCCBP Web Site

The NCCBP Web site (www.nccbp.org) provides detailed information about the project's history, subscribers, benchmarks, timelines, and data collection and subscription process. The site also provides subscribers with password access to compare benchmarks with peer institutions. Subscribers can, in real time, select peers by name or by one or more institutional characteristics (for example, institutional type, enrollment, or operating budget), then select a specific benchmark and immediately receive a report of benchmark values, ranked from highest to lowest within the selected peer group. Comparisons are reported confidentially: the subscriber's institution is identified by name, but peers are identified by letter only. Exhibit 7.1 is an example of a peer-comparison report for the "next-term persistence" benchmark.

**Exhibit 7.1. Example Peer Comparison
Report for Next-Term Persistence**

A	74%
B	69%
C	68%
D	68%
Subscriber	66%
F	60%
G	58%
H	50%

Project Enhancements

The NCCBP is an evolving data collection and reporting system that enables participants to compare themselves on commonly defined benchmarks. From aggregate data and peer comparisons, participants can answer important "compared-to-whom" questions; they can also rank themselves among peer institutions to identify strengths and weaknesses and to prioritize improvement activities. Although comparative analyses tell institutions where they stand relative to peers, they do not identify best practices and processes associated with top-performing colleges. Even though we recognize needs for data confidentiality, future implementations of the project will attempt to facilitate exchange of best practices information by, perhaps, identifying top performers on subsets of benchmarks.

Also, as needs for additional outcomes and indicators are recognized (for example, fiscal and social responsibility indicators), new data elements and benchmarks will be incorporated into NCCBP's flexible data collection and reporting system.

Uses of NCCBP Data

The NCCBP has established an efficient data collection and reporting mechanism that provides a wide range of information to use in a variety of strategic planning and quality improvement efforts. Current participants use aggregate results and peer comparisons to advise local quality improvement initiatives and accreditation requirements. For example, NCCBP data are used for benchmarking requirements by colleges participating in the Higher Learning Commission of the North Central Association's Academic Quality Improvement Program (AQIP), and in the Southern Association of Colleges and Schools' Quality Enhancement Plan (QEP). NCCBP data may also address requirements for quality awards (for example, the Malcolm Baldrige National Quality Award). NCCBP benchmarks have also been incorporated into the Tennessee Higher Education System's performance funding model. In addition, participants use comparative data provided by the NCCBP for institutional program reviews and assessment initiatives and in discussions of problems such as low course retention and graduation rates. In summary, the NCCBP has established a process by which community colleges can systematically collect data and make comparisons to peer institutions that can inform strategic decision making, improve quality, and demonstrate institutional effectiveness.

RALPH JUHNKE is senior research analyst in the Office of Institutional Research at Johnson County Community College in Overland Park, Kansas, and assistant director of the National Community College Benchmark Project.

NEW DIRECTIONS FOR COMMUNITY COLLEGES • DOI: 10.1002/cc

8

This chapter discusses how Central Piedmont Community College (CPCC) has used data from the National Community College Benchmark Project. Analysis of project benchmark data led to a review of high course-withdrawal rates and CPCC withdrawal policies as well as their effects on student program completion and within-term retention. As a result, the college implemented a volunteer pilot study to attempt to lower withdrawal rates through the use of creative classroom strategies.

Using Benchmark and Assessment Data to Facilitate Institutional Change

Terri M. Manning, Brad Bostian

Central Piedmont Community College (CPCC) is a large, urban community college located in Charlotte, North Carolina. CPCC is one of fifty-eight community colleges in the North Carolina Community College System and enrolls approximately twenty-four thousand students in credit-bearing courses each year. In the late 1990s, a number of CPCC faculty and staff had become concerned about an apparent high course-withdrawal rate at the college, although several others perceived the college's rate as similar to the national average. After attempting to track down the "national average" for withdrawal rates, however, we learned that no such data existed. We contacted several colleges of comparable size across the country for comparative purposes, but withdrawal rates were not defined or measured consistently across institutions, making comparisons impossible.

Withdrawal and retention rates can be measured and defined in many ways. Some institutions address *within-term retention,* or the percentage of students who earn a grade versus the percentage who withdraw from or drop one or more of their classes over the course of a term. By this definition, if a student takes four classes and withdraws from one, she was retained in 75 percent of her courses. Community colleges might compare retention rates across all courses, in remedial courses, or in key gateway courses, such as English, college algebra, and biology. Other institutions define retention as a percentage of the student headcount that is retained fully or partially to the end of the term, or they count the percentage of students who withdraw from all of their classes and exit the college. By these

NEW DIRECTIONS FOR COMMUNITY COLLEGES, no. 134, Summer 2006 © Wiley Periodicals, Inc.
Published online in Wiley InterScience (www.interscience.wiley.com) • DOI: 10.1002/cc.239

definitions, if a college has 25,000 students and 2,500 withdraw from all their courses and exit the college, the institution has a 90 percent within-term retention rate and a 10 percent withdrawal rate. Many colleges study institutional records of the students who withdraw in order to determine the courses in which the students were enrolled when they dropped out. By making improvements in these courses, the college may be able to improve retention rates significantly.

Central Piedmont uses both of these definitions of retention. In 2003 and 2004 approximately 14 percent of students withdrew from all their classes and exited the college, and approximately 22 percent of all course registrations ended in a withdrawal. Students who exited all their courses and left the college, termed "walk-aways" by CPCC faculty and staff, have different characteristics than other students at the college, even those who enroll in multiple classes and withdraw from one or more over the course of the term. While both groups of students may not be adequately prepared or may have enrolled in too many courses, walk-aways are more likely to have a major life event influence them to drop out completely. In examining institutional records of these walk-away students, we learned that many do not just withdraw from all of their courses once, but rather do so repeatedly.

Discussion and speculation about CPCC students' persistence and withdrawal rates came to a head in spring 2003, when the college was invited to participate as a pilot institution in the National Community College Benchmark Project (NCCBP), sponsored by Johnson County Community College in Overland Park, Kansas. One of the important benchmarks in the NCCBP database deals with student course-withdrawal rates; based on the pilot data, CPCC had the highest withdrawal rates of all the colleges in the pilot year of the project, as shown in Table 8.1.

This finding came as an unwelcome shock to many at the college but confirmed the suspicions of those who thought that CPCC's course-withdrawal rates were unusually high. Both groups, however, saw this infor-

Table 8.1. Grade Distributions and Course Withdrawal Rates Among NCCBP Pilot Colleges, by Percentage of Students

	All NCCP Pilot Colleges			
Grade	Minimum	Median	Maximum	CPCC
A	26	33.4	45	26.1
B	18	23.3	27	21.1
C	6	13.9	17	12.7
D	1	4	8	3.5
F	2	4.9	15	6.7
W	1	16.2	29.9	29.9

mation as a potentially valuable lever with which to initiate changes in the ways CPCC interacts with and serves students, both inside and outside the classroom. After a brief discussion about the institutional and student characteristics that contribute to withdrawal and retention in community colleges, this chapter describes a volunteer pilot intervention that was instituted in response to data from the National Community College Benchmark Project. The chapter also identifies changes that need to be addressed in order to improve student retention at CPCC.

Factors Contributing to Community College Withdrawal Rates

In order to understand a student's decision to withdraw and to create successful interventions to encourage them not to, colleges must look at all the possible factors that contribute to the behavior. Some of the factors relate to institutional characteristics, such as college policies, faculty attitudes, and tuition rates, and some relate to student characteristics, such as academic preparation, educational experience, and level of commitment to their courses.

Institutional Characteristics. Numerous institutional factors affect student persistence and withdrawal in community colleges. For example, two-year colleges frequently have liberal withdrawal policies in comparison to four-year colleges and universities. At CPCC, students may withdraw from their classes without penalty until the end of the twelfth week of a sixteen-week semester. In comparison, most four-year institutions do not allow withdrawal after the first few weeks of the term. Liberal withdrawal policies may contribute to high withdrawal and low retention rates at CPCC. Figure 8.1 depicts withdrawal patterns during the fall 2000 semester at CPCC. As shown in this figure, most CPCC students persist until midterm (week eight), but after this point withdrawal rates begin to increase much more steeply. By the twelfth-week withdrawal-without-penalty deadline in fall 2000, 15.2 percent of CPCC students had withdrawn from one or more of their classes; 26.2 percent had withdrawn by the end of the semester.

Low tuition rates in North Carolina community colleges may also contribute to student attrition. Because in-state tuition is only $38 per credit hour, with a maximum of $608 per term (North Carolina has the second-lowest community college tuition in the United States), the relatively low price of retaking a class may be a factor in CPCC's high withdrawal rate. Some facets of the organization's culture may also contribute to student withdrawal. Prior to 1990, CPCC only awarded grades of A, B, C, incomplete, and withdraw; no students received Ds or Fs. This grading process essentially forced students to withdraw from classes if they were not doing at least C-level work. Because many faculty and staff who were at CPCC before 1990 are still at the college, there seems to be a somewhat laissez-faire attitude in regard to student withdrawals. For years students have been

Figure 8.1. CPCC Withdrawal Pattern, Fall 2000

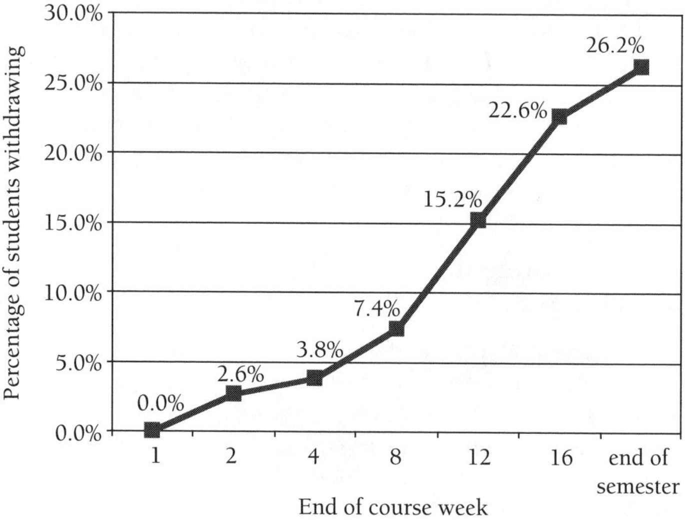

Note: Data based on 39,946 registrations.

encouraged by classmates, faculty, and staff to withdraw from classes if they are doing poorly rather than receive a D or F.

Student Characteristics. In addition to institutional factors, many student characteristics affect whether or not students will withdraw from one or all classes. Clearly, academic variables such as grades, placement test scores, educational achievement, and academic preparation are related to retention and withdrawal (Sandiford and Jackson, 2003). However, researchers point to other student variables that relate to retention as well, including ethnicity (Baldwin, 2002; Johnson and Molnar, 1996), campus involvement (Astin, 1993; Crawford, 1999), transitions to college and freshman orientation courses (Dale, 1995; Derby and Smith, 2004; Hodum and Martin, 1994; Pomalaza-Raez and Groff, 2003), clear educational objectives (Goel, 2002; Walters, 2003), accountability systems (Hanushek and Raymond, 2004), financial aid (Singell, 2001), student support services (Harter, 2000), access to technology and physical facilities (Lau, 2003), and even students' learning styles and the level of their father's education (Vare, Dewalt, and Dockery, 2000).

It is also easy to imagine how students may become accustomed to lenient withdrawal policies and therefore not commit early in the semester to completing a class successfully. Indeed, they may adopt a "wait and see" philosophy, thinking that if they are not doing well by midterm, they can drop the class. Analysis of enrollment patterns at CPCC suggested that students shop around for classes and often drop and add multiple courses before they settle into a schedule. This attitude also encourages students to enroll in some courses at the last minute, often after the term has begun and they have missed multiple class sessions.

Many community college students also face multiple environmental and personal barriers, and how well the institution integrates students socially and academically can contribute to retention (Tinto, 1993). However, community colleges typically do not have dorms, have few active student clubs and organizations, and many students are too busy working to take advantage of available opportunities for co-curricular involvement. Given these barriers, CPCC decided that the best ways to decrease student withdrawal rates were to improve support systems, policies, and classroom practices.

It is clear that retention and success in courses are inseparable—if students do not attend class, they will not succeed in that class. An important component of student commitment is self-efficacy, which requires support from others (Bandura, 1997). Self-efficacy in the classroom comes from student success and timely feedback from faculty. When students feel successful and overcome challenges, they usually persist.

The CPCC Solution. Research shows that colleges can foster a sense of community in the classroom by incorporating cooperative learning (Cooper, 1995), maximizing faculty contact with students (Pascarella and Terenzini, 1991), engaging in positive teaching by communicating a belief that the student will succeed (Lau, 2003), and by giving active, authentic assignments where students learn by doing work that reflects the real world (Astin, 1993; Kuh, Pace, and Vesper, 1997). Thus, in spring 2004 CPCC sought faculty volunteers who would be willing to change their classroom activities and perform additional work with at least one section of their course to determine if improvements could be made in course retention. Seven faculty members in the reading, English, and humanities department volunteered to conduct a pilot intervention. Of the courses taught by the faculty who volunteered, eleven sections of six courses were selected to participate in the project to study and improve withdrawal rates on campus. The sections contained 296 students and consisted of remedial English and reading, expository writing, argument-based research, professional research and reporting, and British literature I. While the pilot intervention was not conducted as a research study (using random selection and with strict control of variables), staff in the Office of Planning and Research matched another eleven sections (with 306 students) of the same courses based on time of day and location to act as a comparison group. Faculty volunteers began meeting in fall 2004 and agreed on a set of conditions for the target sections. First, students would be required to sign a release form agreeing to participate in the study. If they refused, they were moved to a non-target course (few students declined to participate). Second, students in the target courses would not be allowed to withdraw from any course during spring 2005 without first getting the permission of the instructor. If a student wanted to withdraw from a course, the faculty member would offer assistance or additional help to keep them in the class as long as possible.

In addition, faculty in the pilot sections agreed to present a number of new pieces of information on the first day of the semester. They provided an orientation, giving students information about the writing center, tutors, and librarians, as well as other resources to facilitate their success; they instituted a formal attendance policy; and they held a realistic discussion about the value of the skills to be learned in the course. They also distributed a syllabus that included a description of authentic assignments and course policies and provided students with a statement about the faculty member's teaching philosophy and their belief in students' ability to be successful in the course. During the first weeks of the course, faculty constructed minicommunities (groups of three to five students who traded contact information, called one another when someone was absent, and participated in peer editing and group assignments and activities). Over the course of the term, faculty held conferences with each student to discuss their needs and progress in the course, contacted students if they missed class, welcomed back and reintegrated students who had been absent, engaged in positive teaching by trying to involve each student in every class and by structuring assignments that ensured continual student success, and provided active, authentic assignments. During the semester faculty teaching the target courses kept in touch with each other and contacted other support staff, such as counselors, admissions officers, and planning and research staff when needed.

Findings

Far fewer withdrawals were posted for students in the target sections (21 out of 296, or 7.1 percent) than in either the comparison sections (46 out of 306, or 15.0 percent) or the entire Reading, English, and Humanities Department (977 out of 7,207, or 13.6 percent). Students in the target sections also had lower withdrawal rates in their other classes (154 out of 1,401, or 11.0 percent) than did students in comparison sections (232 out of 1,508, or 15.4 percent).

In terms of overall grades in English courses, students in the target sections were more successful (72.7 percent passed the class with a grade of D or better) than those in the comparison sections (66.7 percent). Students in the target sections also had 5.3 percent fewer unsuccessful grades (Fs, incompletes, and withdrawals) than those in the comparison sections. Steps were also taken to determine the percentage of students from both groups who withdrew from all their classes and walked away from the college. We found that 7.3 percent of students in the pilot sections withdrew from all their classes and walked away from the college, compared to 10 percent of students in the comparison groups. Success rates for participating instructors were also revealing. The three-year (2002–2004) passing rate for the instructors of the comparison sections was 69.7 percent; during the pilot intervention it was 2 percent lower. The three-year success rate for the target group instructors was slightly lower at 66.6 percent; that rate increased by 6 percent during the pilot study.

Conclusions

The strategies faculty members in target course sections used during this study appear to have had a noticeable effect on student withdrawals. Fewer students in the pilot sections withdrew from courses, fewer were unsuccessful (earning F, incomplete, or withdrawal grades), and fewer withdrew from all their courses and walked away from the college. Tinto (1993) noted that colleges are not doing the things they need to do to maximize student integration and therefore retention and success. He also suggested that we could only expect incremental gains, because larger gains are not possible without significant changes to an institution. However, we believe that even incremental gains are worthwhile. If the incremental gains that were observed in this study were extended throughout the college, they would result in 2,400 more completions each semester. But extending the gains across the college would carry with it a price for faculty and student services staff. Faculty members would have to agree to change their teaching strategies, alter classroom activities, and engage students outside the classroom. In community colleges where the teaching load is already high, this could prove to be too much for many faculty members. Student services staff would have to work closely with faculty to intervene in the lives of students who are trying to withdraw from classes. Instead of automatically processing withdrawals, they would have to take the time to send students back to their faculty members to obtain assistance or to a trained counselor who could advise them on personal issues.

CPCC's next steps are to expand the withdrawal intervention to include additional departments, carefully select faculty based on historic success rates (the percentage of students making A, B, or C grades in courses) to do a more scientific study of the effect of the teaching strategies on student success, and then, if the first two steps are successful, to offer professional development opportunities to faculty to help them develop classroom strategies to improve retention.

Prior to participating in the National Community College Benchmark Project, many CPCC faculty and staff were living in a state of benign ignorance regarding student withdrawal rates, relying on a culture of anecdote rather than a culture of evidence in their assumptions that CPCC student withdrawal rates were comparable to those of other community colleges. NCCBP peer comparison data served as a surprising wake-up call and can be credited with motivating college faculty and staff to initiate and implement strategies that were subsequently demonstrated to be effective in reducing course-withdrawal rates.

As a result of the findings of this pilot project to improve CPCC's withdrawal rates, many institutional changes are being considered, including modifying course-withdrawal policies (specifically, instituting earlier withdraw deadlines), providing additional support services for students and training for faculty, and modifying classroom activities and procedures to mimic those used in the pilot project. None of these changes would have occurred without CPCC's participation in the NCCBP. Being able to compare CPCC's withdrawal rates (and other valid, reliable, national benchmarks) to those at peer institutions allowed the college to improve teaching, learning, planning, and institutional management.

References

Astin, A. *What Matters in College? Four Critical Years Revisited.* San Francisco: Jossey-Bass, 1993.

Baldwin, A. *Retention Rate by Ethnicity.* Report no. 2002–17C. Miami, Fla.: Miami Dade College, Office of Institutional Research, 2002. (ED 482 591)

Bandura, A. *Self-Efficacy: The Exercise of Control.* New York: W. H. Freeman, 1997.

Cooper, M. M. "Cooperative Learning: An Approach for Large Enrollment Courses." *Journal of Chemical Education,* 1995, *72,* 162.

Crawford, L. *Extended Opportunity Programs and Services for Community College Retention.* Paper presented at the 8th annual California Community College conference, Monterey, Calif., March 1999. (ED 429 642)

Dale, P. M. *A Successful College Retention Program.* West Lafayette, Ind.: Purdue University, 1995. (ED 380 017)

Derby, D., and Smith, T. "An Orientation Course and Community College Retention." *Community College Journal of Research and Practice,* 2004, *28*(9), 763–773.

Goel, M. *Educational Objectives and Retention at Two Community Colleges.* Paper presented at the 42nd annual meeting of the Association for Institutional Research, Toronto, Ontario, Canada, June 2002. (ED 468 770)

Hanushek, E. A., and Raymond, M. E. *Does School Accountability Lead to Improved Student Performance?* NBER Working Paper no. 10591. Cambridge, Mass.: National Bureau of Economic Research, 2004. http://www.nber.org/papers/w10591. Accessed Feb. 14, 2006.

Harter, J. L. *Summary of the P.A.S.S. Program (Project Assuring Student Success).* Toledo: Mercy College of Northwest Ohio, 2000. (ED 452 886)

Hodum, R. L., and Martin, O. L. *An Examination of College Retention Rates with a University 101 Program.* Paper presented at the annual meeting of the Mid-South Education Research Association, Nashville, Tenn., Nov. 1994. (ED 380 036)

Johnson, M. M., and Molnar, D. *Comparing Retention Factors for Anglo, Black, and Hispanic Students.* Paper presented at the annual meeting of the Association for Institutional Research, Albuquerque, N. M., May 1996.

Kuh, G. D., Pace, C. R., and Vesper, N. "The Development of Process Indicators to Estimate Students' Gains Associated with Good Practices in Undergraduate Education." *Research in Higher Education,* 1997, *38*(4), 435–454.

Lau, L. K. "Institutional Factors Affecting Student Retention." *Education,* 2003, *124*(1), 126–136.

Pascarella, E., and Terenzini, P. *How College Affects Students: Findings and Insights from Twenty Years of Research.* San Francisco: Jossey-Bass, 1991.

Pomalaza-Raez, C., and Groff, B. H. "Retention 101: Where Robots Go . . . Students Follow." *Journal of Engineering Education,* 2003, January, 1–6. http://users.ipfw.edu/groff/09-EE015–02–2033.pdf. Accessed Feb. 14, 2006.

Sandiford, J. R., and Jackson, D. K. *Predictors of First Semester Attrition and Their Relation to Retention of Generic Associate Degree Nursing Students.* Paper presented at the annual meeting of the Council for the Study of Community Colleges, Dallas, Tex., April 2003. (ED 481 947)

Singell, L. D., Jr. *Come and Stay a While: Does Financial Aid Affect Enrollment and Retention at a Large Public University?* Ithaca, N.Y.: Cornell University, Cornell Higher Education Research Institute, 2001. (ED 482 386)

Tinto, V. *Leaving College: Rethinking the Causes and Cures of Student Attrition.* Chicago: University of Chicago Press, 1993.
Vare, J. W., Dewalt, M. W., and Dockery, E. R. *Predicting Student Retention in Teacher Education Programs.* Paper presented at the 52nd annual meeting of the American Association of Colleges for Teacher Education, Chicago,Feb. 2000. (ED 482 386)
Walters, E. "Perking Up Retention Rates." *Community College Week,* 2003, *15*(21), 4.

TERRI M. MANNING is associate vice president for institutional research at Central Piedmont Community College in Charlotte, North Carolina.

BRAD BOSTIAN is discipline chair for developmental English at Central Piedmont Community College in Charlotte, North Carolina.

9

This chapter distinguishes between benchmarks and benchmarking, describes a number of data and cultural limitations to benchmarking projects, and suggests that external demands for accountability are the dominant reason for growing interest in benchmarking among community colleges.

Limitations of Community College Benchmarking and Benchmarks

Trudy H. Bers

Chapters in this volume of *New Directions for Community Colleges* demonstrate the growing interest in and use of benchmarking studies in community colleges. Driven by both external and internal demands for data that enable institutions to evaluate how they are doing compared to peer colleges, these studies are becoming the coin of the realm in demonstrating that institutions are self-reflective, non-parochial, and data-driven. However, community college benchmarking studies that move beyond a single state are still relatively novel. While they hold strong potential for improving management, resource allocation, and student achievement, and can help meet accreditation and accountability reporting requirements, benchmarking studies have limitations that need to be understood and taken into consideration. The purpose of this chapter is to identify some of these limitations. I do not wish to tarnish or undermine benchmarking, but to make visible the potential pitfalls that may erode the credibility, validity, and utility of benchmarking projects.

My perspective is national. That is, I recognize that within a state system, many benchmarking projects are driven by a system-level agency that has the authority to make decisions about data definitions, standards, tabulation algorithms, and methods of analysis. Ordinarily, staff at the system level work with institutional researchers or other college administrators to shape data collection activities in order to ensure that they are feasible and so that colleges share a common understanding of what is expected. Though I am not so naïve as to assert that every institution within a system does

New Directions for Community Colleges, no. 134, Summer 2006 © Wiley Periodicals, Inc.
Published online in Wiley InterScience (www.interscience.wiley.com) • DOI: 10.1002/cc.240

things in an identical way—even when they mean to do so—I do contend that the difficulties of designing and implementing benchmarking projects are greater for institutions across states than within a state. Thus, some of what I have to say may be less salient for intra-state studies.

Benchmarking and Benchmarks

Before discussing limitations, it is critical to differentiate between two different terms that are often interchanged: benchmarking and benchmarks.

Benchmarking. Quoting Kempner (1993), Alstete (1995) describes benchmarking as an "ongoing, systematic process for measuring and comparing the work processes of one organization to those of another, by bringing an external focus to internal activities, functions, or operations" (n.p.). Alstete goes on to say that the "goal of benchmarking is to provide key personnel in charge of processes with an external standard for measuring the quality and cost of internal activities, and to help identify where opportunities for improvement may reside." This definition of benchmarking focuses on the examination of processes rather than a specific quantitative measure or indicator. Benchmarking in this way enables one institution to learn how another institution does its work and then determine if and how the first institution can adopt or adapt the processes of the second.

Benchmarking can also be understood as the process of comparing quantitative indicators about a particular topic, such as graduation rates or the percentage of students who move from remedial to college-level work, at peer institutions. In this definition the emphasis is on the activities involved in compiling comparable data about a topic and discussing the findings to help an institution evaluate its own performance in light of its peers' performance.

Benchmark. A benchmark is a metric or a standard, such as the percentage of credits taught by full-time faculty, or the percentage of students who score at a stipulated level on a standardized test. A benchmark may be a threshold or a minimum achievement that is acceptable. A benchmark may also be aspirational, such as a goal an institution seeks to reach. Or a benchmark may define the norm, such as the average of peer institutions on a certain measure.

A benchmark may be identified so as to help the institution determine improvement. For example, a college might measure what percentage of students who place into remedial mathematics pass a college-level math course within three years. The institution may then revise its math curriculum, add support services, change its test cutoff scores for course placement, and take other measures in order to improve student performance. After implementing these or other revisions, an institution can see whether the percentage of students passing college-level math courses has increased over the baseline benchmark.

Connecting Benchmarking and Benchmarks. My reason for defining benchmarking and benchmarks is to highlight that, although they are related, each emphasizes a different aspect of the comparative process. Benchmark-

ing is an activity, and it can focus on the ways in which an institution organizes, communicates, funds operations, evaluates accomplishments, makes
changes, and otherwise provides programs and services, whether these be
instructional, student support, or business operations. Benchmarks are quantitative measures that reflect an institution's performance but do not provide
insights into what influenced that performance. They do permit one institution to compare itself to another, or to a group of colleges, but do not provide clues about what the institution might do to improve.

Limitations of Data

The limitations noted in this section relate primarily to the use of benchmarks, not to benchmarking. They deal with issues associated with defining, collecting, and making meaning of data.

Data Definitions and Standards. When comparing data across colleges about what are putatively the same measures, significant misinterpre-
tations can be made if data definitions and standards are not the same.
Colleges face many challenges with respect to data definitions and standards. One challenge is to define a data element clearly; for example, who
is a "new" student? Another is to collect and code raw data consistently to
align with the definition. The use of the Web for many transactions has
exacerbated this challenge by distancing and enlarging the number of individuals who enter data directly into the system, although providing check-
off screens for commonly used values may help. A third challenge is to
ensure that those who collect or use data share a common understanding.

Let me give two examples. First, in Illinois many non-credit courses
receive state apportionment. By "non-credit" I mean courses that are not eligible for financial aid and do not count in determining whether an individual is a part-time or full-time student; at many schools these courses are
referred to as continuing education. Some individuals at my college use the
term "credit" course to refer to courses that are eligible for financial aid,
including remedial courses. Other individuals at my institution use the term
credit to refer to all courses eligible for state apportionment. Thus, questions
about the number of credit courses or the number of students enrolled in
credit courses may be answered very differently depending on whose definition of credit is applied.

A second example has to do with number of credits taught during a
semester. Again, this example is from Illinois, and from my own institution
in particular. Illinois's apportionment is based on midterm credit hours, but
tuition and fee calculations and faculty workload measures are ordinarily
based on data from the date refunds are no longer issued or on the official
census date. When my business office talks about credits, they typically
refer to the apportionment (midterm) count, but when researchers and faculty talk about credit hours, they most often refer to the census date. With
withdrawals of 10 percent or more between the census date and midterm,

numbers can shift dramatically. Whose data are correct? Both, but with different definitions. A key to using the credit-hour count as a benchmark is to know which count is being used and then to find a comparable count at other institutions. Within the state, the apportionment counts should be comparable among community colleges because we operate under the same state rules regarding state reimbursement. And we also submit our credit-hour counts as of the official census date, so the census date credit-hour counts ought to be comparable as well. But do other states use the same systems? If we benchmark our credit hours as of the midterm date against credit hours at another college that uses their census date counts, are we comparing responsibly? The answer is obvious.

Funding Differences Across States. States vary in the ways community colleges are funded; for example, in some states local property taxes comprise a substantial revenue source for two-year institutions, whereas in other states all public funds are received from the state. For many benchmark subjects, funding may not matter, but for others, funding variations may influence programs and services. For example, in states that provide differential funding by discipline, colleges may seek to maximize enrollments in courses that draw high revenue and limit enrollments in those that produce low revenue. Comparing course offerings by discipline might reveal substantial differences across institutions, but the cause for the differences may not be so apparent. Often such differences are presumed to reflect a combination of student demand and institutional mission, but the powerful effect of differential funding may not be evident. It would behoove an institution comparing itself to out-of-state colleges to investigate funding formulas to assess whether they affect the measures being examined.

Statewide Contracts and Regulations That Limit Institutional Flexibility. Some states—Minnesota and Massachusetts, for example—have statewide faculty contracts. The contracts limit an institution's ability to set salaries, benefits, and various working conditions. While comparisons with institutions in other states might help to make the case for changes in state contracts and regulations, such comparisons will be of limited value in helping a single school address weaknesses. In some ways, the creation of statewide regulations might actually strengthen the value of benchmarks. For example, if a state requires all colleges to use the same placement tests and cutoff scores, comparisons of students' performance in remedial and gatekeeper courses might be more meaningful than comparisons with schools that use a variety of placement approaches.

Labor Contracts and Institutional Practices That Limit Intra-Institutional Flexibility. This limitation is related to the preceding one, but it is imposed by decisions made at the institutional level regarding salaries and benefits. Community colleges often establish criteria for determining entry-level salaries based on factors such as years of teaching experience, advanced degrees, industry experience, and regional or national supply and demand for faculty in a particular discipline. Colleges may also

New Directions for Community Colleges • DOI: 10.1002/cc

have articulated criteria for salary advancement; usually these are based on years at the institution and a variety of professional development accomplishments, such as advanced degrees, publications, earning vendor credentials, licensure or certification by external agencies, and presentations at professional conferences. Some institutions will also award salary-advancement credit for institutional service, such as chairing major committees. Two practices common in many four-year colleges and universities—offering a high salary to recruit a specific faculty member from another institution or matching or exceeding an external offer to retain a faculty member—rarely exist in community colleges.

To learn more about the bases for granting faculty raises, I conducted a brief e-mail survey of colleagues on the National Council for Community College Research and Planning listserv. I asked four simple questions: (1) Does your college have a collective bargaining agreement governing compensation for full-time faculty? (2) Do you have a salary schedule for the academic year for full-time faculty? (3) Does your college give raises to full-time faculty based on supply and demand for faculty in the discipline? Put another way, do you give differential salaries based on discipline after the initial hire? (4) Which (of a number of listed) factors are used to determine raises for a full-time faculty member after the initial hire? Fifty-six colleagues from eighteen states and Canada responded.

All but three respondents said their colleges had a collective-bargaining agreement governing compensation, although sixteen said the agreement was de facto rather than de jure. Only four respondents said faculty salaries were individually negotiated. Eight said they had some flexibility to set salaries based on discipline differences. Primary factors influencing raises after hire were years of service ($n = 44$), earning an advanced degree after hire ($n = 42$), earning graduate credits but not a degree after hire ($n = 47$), and to a much lesser extent, earning continuing education units ($n = 9$). Many said faculty had the opportunity to earn additional pay through overloads, summer-school teaching, and occasionally, a stipend for administrative or other work.

The end result of this limitation and the one imposed by statewide agreements is that community college faculty salaries, especially when examined by discipline, only weakly reflect the market. Rather, they are driven by the same factors (such as the cost of living and college wealth) that influence the overall salary schedule, as well as the length of time faculty have been at the institution and any graduate education or professional experiences that are rewarded by the college's salary agreements. Moreover, institutions rarely have the opportunity to intentionally reduce costs within a discipline by constraining faculty raises because raises are typically granted according to institution-wide rather than discipline-based metrics.

Challenges of Measuring "Success." Student success has gained great national prominence in the past few years—witness projects such as Achieving the Dream, which focuses on achievements of community college students, especially minority and low-income students; the National Postsecondary Education Cooperative multipart student success initiative, which includes federally funded grants and research as well as a national symposium in November 2006; and the Foundations of Excellence project to improve the experience of new community college students. The inherent weakness of using graduation rates to measure community college student success is well known and need not be addressed here. What is problematic is to identify other indicators of success that lend themselves to comparable measurement across institutions and states. Conceptually, this is not difficult. We can probably all agree that movement from remedial to college-level courses in mathematics and composition is an indicator of success, that transfer is an indicator of success, and that a job promotion is an indicator of success. What is difficult is obtaining the data and doing so in a way that permits valid comparisons across institutions.

Centralized Budgeting. At many community colleges, budgets for resources such as computer labs, lab assistants, tutors, duplication, and general supplies are centralized. In the absence of strictly applied internal chargeback policies or practices that have consequences for the budget of each unit, there will be few if any attempts to calculate the draw on these resources by disciplines, departments, or administrative units. Thus, measures such as program or unit costs will either be partial, probably based on direct costs such as salaries and benefits of faculty and staff specifically assigned to the program, or will be estimates based on assumptions or occasional studies to assess the proportional amount of a resource used by a specific unit. The validity of unit cost comparisons by discipline or program will decline the more cost data include dollars budgeted centrally and not carefully tracked back to actual program-level expenditures.

Limitations of Culture

The limitations noted above are primarily technical in nature. Though not trivial, they illustrate challenges within the data. The limitations discussed in this section reside more in the culture of the community college as an institution and the receptivity of administrators, faculty, and staff to understanding and discussing data, using data to foster new and reflective thinking about the institution, and making decisions accordingly.

Willingness and Ability to Adopt or Adapt Processes from Another College. This limitation relates to benchmarking rather than to the use of benchmarks. In using benchmarking to understand how another institution organizes, funds, delivers, and evaluates a particular program or service, the community college doing the benchmarking has to be willing to examine its own structures and ways of doing business—including long-time and well-entrenched programs and processes. While the inability to incorporate processes in place at other colleges may be due to resource constraints, it may also be due to political influences, a general resistance to change, and defensiveness in protecting existing turf.

Accepting Surprises. Community colleges, like all institutions, sometimes believe in "truths" that have accumulated over time and become part of the fabric of the college. Perhaps accurately depicting reality in the past, these truths may persist because they are unexamined (either the result of benign neglect or fear of finding that old successes no longer exist).

Examining the New. Sometimes community colleges have simply not thought about examining data about a particular topic, especially through comparisons with other institutions. Community colleges participating in the Achieving the Dream initiative, for example, are required to look at the gaps in achievement among racial and ethnic groups. A number of participating colleges reported they had not previously engaged in this type of study. Though not specifically comparing themselves to other colleges, by having access to more than thirty-five Achieving the Dream schools, each institution has the potential to compare its students' achievements with those of students in other institutions and can talk about ways to improve.

Reporting Rather Than Responding. Enthusiasm for benchmarking, which seems to be growing, may end at the reporting stage, when an institution simply puts forward data without interpreting them. Especially in situations in which a community college engages in benchmarking to satisfy an external reporting requirement, or when it attempts to demonstrate that it uses the data to make decisions, the temptation to simply report numbers is strong. For example, self-study reports might present data from benchmark studies as evidence of using data without explaining how those data were used at the institution to affirm existing practices or to prompt change. For benchmarking to really be effective, however, the institution needs to respond to benchmarking data with changes to improve, and re-measure itself to determine whether interventions had the intended outcomes.

Community Colleges Are Local and Unique. By mission, community colleges are expected to respond to the needs and characteristics of their local communities. In doing so, many schools claim to be unique, even if the programs and services they offer are not very different from those available at scores of other community colleges. This argument suggests that benchmark studies are inappropriate and perhaps even misleading, because no other institutions are "like mine."

Absence of Rankings and Local Recruitment. Few national movements have generated as much controversy and attention in some higher education circles as the national rankings produced by entities such as *U.S. News and World Report* and *Peterson's Guide*. Simultaneously trying to discredit the validity and value of these rankings and at the same time striving to improve their institutions' standing, leaders of many four-year colleges and universities state that college choice decisions are shaped by rankings and information available through the rankings. Community colleges are not part of this competition, primarily because their students often come from the local area. Indeed, some states create financial disincentives for a student to attend a community college outside of his or her home district. And while community colleges might compete with four-year colleges and universities—especially senior-level, open-enrollment institutions—for the same potential students, there has not yet been demand for data comparing two- and four-year colleges so that they could be ranked on the same scales or within the same classification of schools.

Final Comments

As I noted earlier, chapters in this volume of *New Directions for Community Colleges* demonstrate a growing interest in benchmarks and benchmarking among community colleges as well as increased sophistication in benchmark projects. It is my perspective that two motivations are driving this interest. The first is external: the accountability pressure for colleges to demonstrate they are doing the job they claim to be doing, that students are learning, that institutions are economical and efficient, and that local stakeholders are being served responsibly and responsively. The second is internal: an institution's desire to examine itself in order to identify weaknesses, sustain strengths, and improve. Both motivations support benchmarks and benchmarking. I suspect, however, that if the accountability movement were to fade, some of the zeal for benchmarks and benchmarking would fade as well. It is hard for an institution to be reflective when it does not compete widely to retain faculty, recruit and retain students, or build a national reputation.

Community college leaders who want to infuse benchmarking into their institutions' ways of working have a golden opportunity to do so. Benchmarking is new enough among community colleges so they can be innovators or early adopters, helping to shape studies as they mature. External accountability requirements provide additional leverage. And new national projects have created frameworks and procedures so that benchmarking projects do not have to be created from scratch. It will be interesting, ten years from now, to assess whether benchmarks and benchmarking in community colleges were passing fancies or became integrated into standard operating and decision-making procedures.

References

Alstete, J. W. *Benchmarking in Higher Education: Adapting Best Practices to Improve Quality.* ERIC Digest. Los Angeles: University of California, Los Angeles, ERIC Clearinghouse for Community Colleges, 1995. (ED 402 800) http://www.ericdigests.org/1997–3/bench.html. Accessed Jan. 18, 2006.

Kempner, D. E. "The Pilot Years: The Growth of the NACUBO Benchmarking Project." *NACUBO Business Officer*, 1993, 27(6), 21–31.

TRUDY H. BERS *is executive director of institutional research, curriculum, and strategic planning at Oakton Community College in Des Plaines, Illinois.*

10

This chapter reviews resources from scholars, practitioners, and policymakers on benchmarking in community colleges.

Key Resources on Benchmarking in Community Colleges

Caroline Q. Sheldon, Nathan R. Durdella

Benchmarking—in community colleges just as in any other organization—consists of comparing "practices, processes, and outcomes to standards of excellence in a systematic way" (Inger, 1993, p. 1). Benchmarking, according to McGregor and Attinasi (1998), is "an ongoing, systematic process for measuring and comparing the work processes of one organization to those of another by bringing in external focus for internal activities, functions, or operations" (p. 1). The utility of benchmarking in community colleges depends on how practitioners define excellence, establish and adopt standards of performance, and compare performance—both across institutions and within their own colleges. Literature on benchmarking in community colleges ranges from papers documenting best practices at the institutional level to reports on state policy guidelines and studies examining the effectiveness of benchmarking. This volume of *New Directions for Community Colleges* builds on the existing literature to illustrate how community college researchers, practitioners, and policymakers are approaching the tasks of developing, analyzing, and reporting on benchmarking projects across the country.

As this volume demonstrates, benchmarking can be effectively used to improve community college outcomes and performance. However, as Copa and Ammentorp (1998) have argued, benchmarking is "only the starting point for organizational change," (p. viii). Three key components of benchmarking—examining internal processes, searching for best practices at other institutions, and adapting those practices to the home institution—must be

NEW DIRECTIONS FOR COMMUNITY COLLEGES, no. 134, Summer 2006 © Wiley Periodicals, Inc.
Published online in Wiley InterScience (www.interscience.wiley.com) • DOI: 10.1002/cc.241

embraced before change and improvement can take place (Epper, 1999). Thus, while benchmarking may be the starting point, the end point is improved institutional processes, and ultimately, enhanced student learning both inside the classroom and across campus.

This chapter presents resources that can help community college practitioners design, execute, and evaluate benchmarking programs. The first section covers resources for defining the benchmarking process and designing benchmarking programs, including examining internal processes. The next section looks at model applications of benchmarking and assessment practices at institutions. The following section examines how some community college practitioners have adopted benchmarking processes at their institutions, and the chapter concludes with some final thoughts about benchmarking processes and the importance of investigating peers' experiences in establishing effective benchmarks. The resources provided in the chapter can support community college practitioners' efforts to improve their institutions through benchmarking.

Designing Quality Benchmarking Programs and Processes

In recent years, several community college scholars and practitioners have focused on the need to define and recognize quality benchmarking practices. At the same time, most local, state, and regional policymakers have focused their attention on assessing what takes place inside the classroom. Hence, the rise of exit examinations, student learning outcomes, and other measures of instruction and student learning have lent credibility to the perception that institutional quality lies in the intersection of students, instructors, and the curriculum. Although many benchmarking efforts center around instruction and improving student learning, student experiences outside the classroom are just as important (Astin, 1993), and student affairs departments (sometimes called student services departments) are integral to how students navigate the undergraduate experience. Because student affairs professionals manage a range of student services, including counseling, assessment and placement, career and transfer services, and student life, conduct, government, and activities, it is equally important to assess these services and benchmark them against other institutions. The following papers call for institutions to define how they assess students and set benchmarks in both instructional and support areas. All of these studies pay particular attention to quality in developing, testing, and settling on standards for benchmarking processes.

Bender, B. E. "Benchmarking as an Administrative Tool for Institutional Leaders." In B. E. Bender and J. H. Schuh (eds.), *Using Benchmarking to Inform Practice in Higher Education*. New Directions for Higher Education, no. 118. San Francisco: Jossey-Bass, 2002.

In her chapter from this *New Directions for Higher Education* volume, Bender argues that "benchmarking can be enormously useful to influence and shape institutional decisions" (p. 119). Further, she argues that through analyses of best practices from peer institutions and efforts to adapt and develop practices at their own institutions, practitioners can "improve the quality of programs for their own purposes" (p. 119). Bender identifies a number of issues that can arise in the benchmarking process, including anticipating and planning for resistance to change. For community college practitioners—from academic administrators to faculty senate presidents—the need to build consensus through shared governance committees and the reliance on the support of peers are integral to the successful implementation and management of institutional assessment programs.

Alstete, J. W. *Benchmarking in Higher Education: Adapting Best Practices to Improve Quality.* ASHE-ERIC Higher Education Report No. 5. Washington, D.C.: Office of Educational Research and Improvement, 1995.

This ASHE-ERIC Higher Education Report examines general definitions and practices of benchmarking in higher education. Alstete argues that benchmarking goes beyond data collection to "adapting a new approach of continually questioning how processes are performed, seeking out best practices, and implementing new models of operation" (p. viii). He reviews the origins of benchmarking and examines the process in higher education today, noting that institutions frequently use benchmarking to compare performance. However, he demonstrates that benchmarking has many more uses than simply comparing institutional performance and finds that experience in quality management, which many colleges and universities do not have, is needed to implement effective benchmarks. Alstete identifies a benchmarking process that includes planning a study, conducting research and collecting data, analyzing data, and ultimately adopting the findings as benchmarks. The report concludes with detailed recommendations and an outline for conducting a benchmarking study. Community colleges could readily adopt Alstete's benchmarking process with support from institutional researchers and the participation of key faculty members.

Dowd, A. C. *Data Don't Drive: Building a Practitioner-Driven Culture of Inquiry to Assess Community College Performance.* Lumina Research Report. Indianapolis: Lumina Foundation, 2005. http://www.luminafoundation.org/publications/datadontdrive2005.pdf. Accessed Jan. 27, 2006.

This report introduces the concept of a culture of inquiry to assess the value of benchmarking practices for community colleges. A culture of inquiry relates to community college faculty and administrators' efforts to find the best ways to gauge institutional performance through evidence as well as through the interpretation of evidence. Dowd argues that community college faculty and administrators should be at the center of the benchmarking process and identifies three types of benchmarking: performance, diagnostics, and process. Performance benchmarking refers to the "straight-forward though often superficial comparison of performance data" (p. 2), while diagnostic benchmarking works to identify areas for institutional improvement. Process benchmarking involves in-depth comparisons of two or more institutions to isolate the effects of teaching and learning. The purpose of these three approaches is to develop practitioners' skills in judging the standards to use for improvement. For community colleges, Dowd's culture of inquiry could help all college personnel to understand and participate in the institutional assessment process.

Donsky, A. P. *Strategic Planning, Operational Planning, and Measures of Effectiveness: An Integrated Model*. Paper presented at the annual conference of the Southeastern Association for Community College Research, Orlando, Fla., Aug. 1992. (ED 353 026)

Donsky believes that redundancy in various forms of planning and measuring effectiveness is a barrier to efforts at continuous institutional improvement. He reports on the effectiveness of an Integrated Planning and Effectiveness Model (IPEM), which provides those interested in sustaining effectiveness programs with a methodology that eliminates duplication of effort and leads to one document that can demonstrate an institution's effectiveness. The IPEM uses institutional mission as the point of departure for planning and benchmarking processes. The paper also includes a review of planning models and a list of references to help practitioners prepare an institutional assessment and effectiveness campaign.

Ewell, P. T. "Power in Numbers: The Values in Our Metrics." *Change*, 2005, *July/August*, 10–16.

In this piece, Ewell argues that if you are clear about the value and assumptions in your metrics or standards of measurement, you can "create powerful tools to shape sound policies and to mobilize public support for them" (p. 16). Metrics can be most effectively used to benchmark success and institutional improvement if the context within which they are constructed is understood. Accordingly, community college practitioners should consider the processes of adopting and developing benchmarks as an open, transparent dialogue. In the spirit of shared governance, community college leaders can harness the resources of campuswide committees to carry out the initial and ongoing work of benchmarking.

Best Practices from Peer Institutions

Because there are many issues inherent in the design, execution, and evaluation of benchmarking processes, moving from theory to practice can only be accomplished by taking deliberative, prescriptive steps. Although scholarly studies are informative, community college practitioners can learn much from studying the lessons learned by institutions that have worked to adopt and refine standards and practices for benchmarking. For practitioners, reflecting on and writing about their own experiences in navigating benchmarking and assessment processes can be equally insightful. This section identifies resources related to sustaining quality benchmarking systems.

McGregor, E. N., and Attinasi, L. C., Jr. *The Craft of Benchmarking: Finding and Utilizing District-Level, Campus-Level, and Program-Level Standards.* Paper presented at the annual meeting of the Rocky Mountain Association for Institutional Research, Bozeman, Mont., Oct. 1998. (ED 423 014)

In this paper, McGregor and Attinasi define benchmarking, give a history of benchmarking projects in institutions of higher education, and describe the process at Pima Community College (Arizona) of selecting peer institutions with which to compare standards. The paper begins with a history of how benchmarking emerged in the corporate sector, then turns to how higher education adopted the practice in response to pressures to understand not only how institutions of higher education perform but also how they perform in relation to their peers. In the community college context, the issues that arise in selecting peer institutions for comparisons are unique due to sector and institutional characteristics. McGregor and Attinasi explain that because some community colleges are part of multicollege or multicampus districts, they experience the benchmarking process differently. The authors describe the processes of finding peer institutions appropriate for benchmarking using national databases such as the Integrated Postsecondary Education Data System (IPEDS). Practitioners can select institutions by analyzing institutional data, through site visits or surveys, or via Internet research.

Resnick, L. B., Nolan, K. J., and Resnick, D. P. "Benchmarking Education Standards." *Educational Evaluation and Policy Analysis,* 1995, *17*(4), 438–461.

Resnick, Nolan, and Resnick argue that standards have become "the currency of education reform efforts in the U.S." (p. 438). The force driving this conversion to a currency of standards is a shift to outcomes-based governance and funding, in which legal and educational systems decide what students should be learning. In the United States, however, the push to adopt standards or benchmarks has been difficult because at many colleges there is a culture of avoiding specificity in outcome criteria and measurements. The New Standards Project, a consortium of states and schools that set out to establish a system of standards for high student achievement, recently turned to their counterparts abroad to examine how they defined their standards and the criteria they used for student achievement. The authors use a comparative case-study method to demonstrate that data collected in France and the Netherlands show that benchmarks should be clearly expressed and based on criteria reinforced through the curriculum. This and other lessons could be easily adopted in American community colleges as part of the push to document student learning outcomes.

Barak, R. J., and Kniker, C. R. "Benchmarking by State Higher Education Boards." In B. E. Bender and J. H. Schuh (eds.), *Using Benchmarking to Inform Practice in Higher Education*. New Directions for Higher Education, no. 118. San Francisco: Jossey-Bass, 2002.

Barak and Kniker define benchmarking as a way to compare both best practices from one institution to the next and a "wide array of management practices by state higher education boards" (p. 93). The authors' focus on this latter definition of benchmarking is a distinguishing feature of the paper, and they describe how state higher education boards use the information gleaned from benchmarking processes. Many state boards have emphasized performance benchmarking, which focuses on institutional quality and performance characteristics. To illustrate this focus, Barak and Kniker detail a case study of the Iowa Board of Regents. In 1998, the board adopted a strategic plan that included results in four key areas: quality, access, diversity, and accountability. Subsequently, representatives from institutions governed by the board defined a set of benchmarks that included instruction, student performance, educational service, faculty performance, diversity, and financing. In addition to the goal of raising performance in the four key areas adopted by the board, Barak and Kniker argue that these standards were meant to make benchmarking more compatible with the missions of member colleges and universities. Community college systems across the United States could adopt the collaborative approach taken by colleges in Iowa and focus their benchmarking and assessment efforts on the same key areas.

Adopting Effective Benchmarking Practices in Community Colleges

From understanding internal processes to examining best practices at peer institutions, practitioners have to develop, adopt, and assess effective benchmarks to ensure institutional improvement. The following papers present studies on practitioners' efforts to advance benchmarking in community colleges. The first paper discusses Howard Community College's experiences in forging a new institutional effectiveness system. The next two papers deal with the assessment of essential but often neglected areas in community college research—vocational education and student services—both of which are likely to figure prominently in the future of the community colleges.

Burrill, D., Leff, B., and Heacock, R. *Three Years and Still Going: Howard Community College's Institutional Effectiveness System.* Paper presented at the 6th annual Summer Institute on Institutional Effectiveness and Student Success, Atlantic City, N.J., June 1994. (ED 370 637)

This paper describes the development and transformation of Howard Community College's institutional effectiveness system. The authors detail the initial implementation of the college's strategic priorities, goals, indicators, and administrative recommendations and actions, then describe various difficulties encountered while developing the system, including skepticism of faculty, lack of understanding by all members of the college community, the importance of ensuring good indicators from which to base decisions, and the problem of having too many indicators of student and institutional success. The authors stress that continuity in benchmarking and institutional effectiveness depends on creating a dynamic system that is responsive to change, communicating with key constituencies, and streamlining data collection and reporting.

Inger, M. "Benchmarking in Education: Tech Prep, A Case in Point." *Institute on Education and the Economy Brief,* 1993, 8(Oct.), 1–4.

In this policy brief Inger describes a way to establish and define standards for successful benchmarking systematically. His first recommendation is to identify and understand the processes and outcomes to benchmark. He also argues that it is important to establish baseline data so that comparisons can be made at subsequent points. Once the processes are identified and the data established, Inger suggests outlining and defining institution-specific benchmarks. In doing so, new efforts to achieve standards can be compared to what the institution is currently doing. Inger argues that the goal of benchmarking is improving institutional processes and outcomes, and states that institutions must not only compare their performance to that of their peers, but must also examine practices within their own organizations. For tech prep programs, Inger finds that the following four program components are well suited for benchmarking: articulation, program assessment, career guidance, and marketing. These fours program components are essential to managing a community college technology or vocational education program. For example, community college managers' efforts to recruit and retain students from high schools and the local workforce are essential to program success. The assessment of these efforts could be enhanced if managers compare their programs with those at peer institutions while also using the program review process at their own institution for further assessment.

Richardson, D. *Changing the Organizational Structure of Nonacademic Departments for Institutional Effectiveness.* Abingdon: Virginia Highlands Community College, 1993. (ED 366 372)

This report describes the institutional assessment activities from the Academic and Instructional Support Services division at Virginia Highlands Community College. This division houses support services units seen in most community colleges, including a library archival and retrieval services unit, a learning lab for assessment, and a support unit for information technology. Richardson describes an institutional assessment process that includes an advisory committee and an academic computing committee, student survey instruments, and an external evaluation. The institutional assessment process focused in particular on organizational practices and aimed to establish clearly defined goals, develop qualitative and quantitative data collection methods to benchmark the extent to which goals are achieved, and use results to improve services.

Concluding Remarks

Given the national trend toward accountability in higher education (Cohen and Brawer, 2003), community colleges will need to continue demonstrating their effectiveness by improving institutional performance and student outcomes. Benchmarking is critical to this process. Comparing one's own performance on key indicators to that of peer institutions is an integral part of demonstrating accountability and improving institutional performance. However, benchmarking with peer institutions is only a starting point. The resources presented in this chapter advance the notion that community college leaders must become experts in developing, implementing, and evaluating effective benchmarks. The resources also provide information and suggestions to help community college practitioners in their efforts toward continuous institutional improvement and accountability.

References

Astin, A. W. *What Matters in College: Four Critical Years Revisited.* San Francisco: Jossey-Bass, 1993.

Cohen, A. M., and Brawer, F. B. *The American Community College* (4th ed.). San Francisco: Jossey-Bass, 2003.

Copa, G. H., and Ammentorp, W. *Benchmarking New Designs for Two-Year Institutions of Higher Education.* Berkeley, Calif.: National Center for Research in Vocational Education, 1998.

Epper, R. M. "Applying Benchmarking to Higher Education." *Change,* 1999, *31*(6), 24–31.

Inger, M. "Benchmarking in Education: Tech Prep, A Case in Point." *Institute on Education and the Economy Brief,* 1993, 8(Oct.), 1–4.

McGregor, E. N., and Attinasi, L. C., Jr. "The Craft of Benchmarking: Finding and Utilizing District-Level, Campus-Level, and Program-Level Standards." Paper presented at the annual meeting of the Rocky Mountain Association for Institutional Research, Bozeman, Mont., Oct. 1998. (ED 423 014)

CAROLINE Q. SHELDON is director of research and planning at Cerritos College in Norwalk, California and a doctoral candidate in higher education and organizational change at UCLA.

NATHAN R. DURDELLA is research analyst at Cerritos College in Norwalk, California and recently completed the requirements for his doctoral degree in higher education and organizational change at UCLA.

INDEX

Back Issue/Subscription Order Form

Copy or detach and send to:

Jossey-Bass, A Wiley Imprint, 989 Market Street, San Francisco CA 94103-1741

Call or fax toll-free: Phone 888-378-2537 6:30AM – 3PM PST; Fax 888-481-2665

Back Issues: Please send me the following issues at $29 each
(Important: please include ISBN number for each issue.)

_____

_____

_____

$ _____   Total for single issues

$ _____   SHIPPING CHARGES: SURFACE   Domestic Canadian

| | First Item | $5.00 | $6.00 |
| | Each Add'l Item | $3.00 | $1.50 |

For next-day and second-day delivery rates, call the number listed above.

Subscriptions   Please __ start __ renew my subscription to *New Directions for Community Colleges* for the year 2____at the following rate:

U.S.	__ Individual $80	__ Institutional $180
Canada	__ Individual $80	__ Institutional $220
All Others	__ Individual $104	__ Institutional $254

Online subscriptions are available too!

**For more information about online subscriptions visit
www.interscience.wiley.com**

$ _____   Total single issues and subscriptions (Add appropriate sales tax for your state for single issue orders. No sales tax for U.S. subscriptions. Canadian residents, add GST for subscriptions and single issues.)

__Payment enclosed (U.S. check or money order only)

__VISA __ MC __ AmEx __ # _____Exp. Date _____

Signature _____ Day Phone _____

__ Bill Me (U.S. institutional orders only. Purchase order required.)

Purchase order # _____
          Federal Tax ID13559302   **GST 89102 8052**

Name _____

Address _____

_____

Phone _____ E-mail _____

For more information about Jossey-Bass, visit our Web site at **www.josseybass.com**

CC128　**From Distance Education to E-Learning: Lessons Along the Way**
Beverly L. Bower, Kimberly P. Hardy
Correspondence, telecourses, and now e-learning: distance education
continues to grow and change. This volume's authors examine what
community colleges must do to make distance education successful,
including meeting technology challenges, containing costs, developing
campuswide systems, teaching effectively, balancing faculty workloads,
managing student services, and redesigning courses for online learning.
Includes case studies from colleges, plus state and regional policy
perspectives.
ISBN:　0-7879-7927-9

CC127　**Serving Minority Populations**
Berta Vigil Laden
Focuses on how colleges with emerging majority enrollments of African
American, Hispanic, American Indian, Asian American and Pacific Islander,
and other ethnically diverse students are responding to the needs—
academic, financial, and cultural—of their increasingly diverse student
populations. Discusses partnerships with universities, businesses,
foundations, and professional associations that can increase access,
retention, and overall academic success for students of color. Covers best
practices from Minority-Serving Institutions, and offers examples for
mainstream community colleges.
ISBN:　0-7879-7790-X

CC126　**Developing and Implementing Assessment of Student Learning
Outcomes**
Andreea M. Serban, Jack Friedlander
Colleges are under increasing pressure to produce evidence of student
learning, but most assessment research focuses on four-year colleges. This
volume is designed for practitioners looking for models that community
colleges can apply to measuring student learning outcomes at the classroom,
course, program, and institutional levels to satisfy legislative and
accreditation requirements.
ISBN:　0-7879-7687-3

CC125　**Legal Issues in the Community College**
Robert C. Cloud
Community colleges must be prepared for lawsuits, federal statutes, court
rulings, union negotiations, and other legal issues that could affect
institutional stability and effectiveness. This volume provides leaders with
information about board relations, tenure and employment, student rights
and safety, disability law, risk management, copyright and technology issues,
and more.
ISBN:　0-7879-7482-X

CC124　**Successful Approaches to Fundraising and Development**
Mark David Milliron, Gerardo E. de los Santos, Boo Browning
This volume outlines how community colleges can tap into financial support
from the private sector, as four-year institutions have been doing. Chapter
authors discuss building community college foundations, cultivating
relationships with the local community, generating new sources of revenue,
fundraising from alumni, and the roles of boards, presidents, and trustees.
ISBN:　0-7879-7283-5

NEW DIREC⋯⋯ ⋯⋯⋯⋯
IS NOW AVAILABLE ONLINE AT WILEY INTERSCIENCE

What is Wiley InterScience?

Wiley InterScience is the dynamic online content service from John Wiley & Sons delivering the full text of over 300 leading scientific, technical, medical, and professional journals, plus major reference works, the acclaimed *Current Protocols* laboratory manuals, and even the full text of select Wiley print books online.

What are some special features of Wiley InterScience?

Wiley InterScience Alerts is a service that delivers table of contents via e-mail for any journal available on Wiley InterScience as soon as a new issue is published online.
Early View is Wiley's exclusive service presenting individual articles online as soon as they are ready, even before the release of the compiled print issue. These articles are complete, peer-reviewed, and citable.
CrossRef is the innovative multi-publisher reference linking system enabling readers to move seamlessly from a reference in a journal article to the cited publication, typically located on a different server and published by a different publisher.

How can I access Wiley InterScience?

Visit http://www.interscience.wiley.com

Guest Users can browse Wiley InterScience for unrestricted access to journal Tables of Contents and Article Abstracts, or use the powerful search engine.
Registered Users are provided with a *Personal Home Page* to store and manage customized alerts, searches, and links to favorite journals and articles. Additionally, Registered Users can view free Online Sample Issues and preview selected material from major reference works.
Licensed Customers are entitled to access full-text journal articles in PDF, with select journals also offering full-text HTML.

How do I become an Authorized User?

Authorized Users are individuals authorized by a paying Customer to have access to the journals in Wiley InterScience. For example, a university that subscribes to Wiley journals is considered to be the Customer. Faculty, staff and students authorized by the university to have access to those journals in Wiley InterScience are Authorized Users. Users should contact their Library for information on which Wiley journals they have access to in Wiley InterScience.

ASK YOUR INSTITUTION ABOUT WILEY INTERSCIENCE TODAY!